from your child's teacher

Helping Your Child Learn to Read, Write, and Speak

by Dr. Robin Bright
with Lisa McMullin
and David Platt

© 1998 FP Hendriks Publishing Ltd.
ALL RIGHTS RESERVED
Permission is granted to the purchaser to reproduce pages from the sections entitled Information at a Glance and Book Lists and to reprint designated portions of the printed text in parent newsletters.

From Your Child's Teacher: Helping Your Child Learn to Read, Write, and Speak
by Dr. Robin Bright with Lisa McMullin and David Platt
ISBN: 0-9682970-3-X

FP Hendriks Publishing Ltd.
4806–53 St.
Stettler, AB T0C 2L2
Fax/Phone: (403) 742-6483
Toll Free Fax/Phone: 1-888-374-8787
E-mail: hendriks@telusplanet.net
Website: www.telusplanet.net/public/hendriks

Canadian Cataloguing in Publication Data
Bright, Robin M., 1957–
    From your child's teacher

ISBN 0-9682970-3-X

    1. Early childhood education—Parent participation. 2. Education, Pre-school—Parent participation. 3. Education, Elementary—Parent participation. 4. Language acquisition—Parent participation. I. Lisa McMullin, 1953- II. Platt, David Ian, 1954-. Title.
LB1139.5.L35B74 1998   649'.58   C98-910310-2

Production Team
Thanks to all those talented people who worked on this project:
Authors   Dr. Robin Bright, Lisa McMullin,
                     David Platt
Project Director   Faye Boer
Editors   Faye Boer, Barb Demers
Photos   Hank Boer, Dawn King-Hunter
Cartoons   Sara Carstairs
Draft Preparation   Kelly Corey, Margaret Joblonkay

Manufacturers: Transcontinental Press; Screaming Color;
                Print Stop Inc.
                PRINTED IN CANADA
2nd printing, 1999

Table of Contents

Foreword by Senator Joyce Fairbairn — 1

Introduction: Why this Book Was Conceived — 3

Section One: Reading and Books — 7

Chapter One:	When to Begin	8
Chapter Two:	How to Read with Your Child	11
	Birth to Two Years	11
	Ages Three to Six	13
	Ages Seven to Ten	16
	Ages Eleven and Up	17
Chapter Three:	How Children Learn to Read	22
Chapter Four:	What the Teacher Does and Why	29
Chapter Five:	What to Read	34
	Birth to Two Years	34
	Ages Three to Six	35
	Ages Seven to Ten	37
	Ages Eleven and Up	39
Chapter Six:	What You May Be Concerned About (Questions and Answers)	42

Section Two: Writing—All Children Do It — 49

Chapter Seven:	How Children Learn About Writing	50
Chapter Eight:	How Children Learn to Write	56
Chapter Nine:	What the Teacher Does and Why	65
Chapter Ten:	I Want My Child to Be a Good Speller	69
Chapter Eleven:	Encouraging Daily Writing	74
Chapter Twelve:	What You May Be Concerned About (Questions and Answers)	79

Section Three: Talking, Listening, and Learning — 85

Chapter Thirteen:	From Baby Babble to (Almost) Intelligible Conversation	86

table of contents

Section Three: Talking, Listening, and Learning, continued

Chapter Fourteen:	Daily Activities to Encourage Speech Development	92
Chapter Fifteen:	What the Teacher Does and Why	99
Chapter Sixteen	What You May Be Concerned About (Questions and Answers)	104

Wrapping Up—What We Have Learned 109

Section Four: Information At a Glance (reproducibles) 111

Appendix 1:	When To Begin	112
Appendix 2:	Helpful Reading Hints (Birth to Two Years)	113
Appendix 3:	Helpful Reading Hints (Ages Three to Six)	114
Appendix 4:	Helpful Reading Hints (Ages Seven to Ten)	115
Appendix 5:	Helpful Reading Hints (Ages Eleven and Up)	116
Appendix 6:	Stuck on a Word? Steps to Help Your Child	117
Appendix 7:	Stages of Writing Development	118
Appendix 8:	Helping Children Develop As Writers	119
Appendix 9:	The Writing Process	120
Appendix 10:	Encouraging Daily Writing	121
Appendix 11:	Daily Activities to Encourage Speech Development	122
Appendix 12:	Conversation Starter Hints	123
Appendix 13:	Books About Teaching Spelling	124
Appendix 14:	Professional References	125

Section Five: Book Lists for Children and Young Adults 127

Birth to Two Years	128
Ages Three to Six	133
Ages Seven to Ten	139
Ages Eleven and up	145

The Authors 151

Workshop and Order Information 152

From Your Child's Teacher

Dedications

Each of the authors has dedicated this book to people and ideals that have made a difference in their lives.

I would like to dedicate this book to my mom and dad, my first teachers.

—Robin

I would like to dedicate my efforts on this book to a bountiful supply of love and compassion on the planet so that all people may be fed, have shelter, be safe, and experience joy.

—Lisa

I would like to dedicate this book to the loving memory of Matthew A. Phillips, a lifelong learner, hero, and friend. I would also like to thank my wife, Shari, and my two inspirations, Stacey and Ashley.

—David

Foreword
by
Senator Joyce Fairbairn

This is a book about our future as a country.

It is about children who face lives dominated by the pressures of instant technology and constant change. It is about teaching them to relish the challenge and joy of learning.

Each of us today is guided by the necessity of lifelong learning. And yet, for more than 40 per cent of our adult citizens, some seven million people, this is an enormous struggle.

Because of the varying degrees of difficulty with basic literacy skills—reading, writing, numeracy—far too many are forced to the sidelines, unable to participate fully in our national life. That affects the future health, happiness, and productivity not only of individuals and families but also a whole country.

This book gives us a vision and a practical direction to break that cycle so that all our children will have a fair chance to learn, to succeed in an exciting new century where they will be the leaders of this special nation.

Lifelong learning means exactly what it says. You begin at the start, just as soon as a baby listens and the smallest child is able to turn a page, focus on a picture, or recognize words in a good story.

Each parent is that first, most important teacher, who leads a child into the broader world of education where the greatest achievement comes from a powerful three-way partnership of parent, teacher, and child.

It is a partnership which shields against future problems by instilling in children a sense of fun and excitement and security in learning so they will have a good start today.

I offer my profound thanks to our three authors of *From Your Child's Teacher: Helping Your Child Learn to Read, Write, and Speak* who, as parents, teachers, and friends, have produced a book which will truly change lives.

Joyce Fairbairn
Special Advisor for Literacy
The Senate of Canada

Our Thanks

We wish to thank Senator Fairbairn for her comments and for her work in promoting literacy programs. We offer this book in the hope that all children may benefit in their pursuit of literacy.

We also wish to thank family, friends, and colleagues for allowing their photos and writing to appear in this book. These include;

Brooke Bowles	Teresa Bowles
Zachary Bowles	Amy Bright
Erin Bright	Geraldine Dennis
Aaryn Lynham	Suzanne McMullin
Tim McMullin	Lisa McMullin
Anne Pinder	Joanne Pinder
Katherine Pinder	Neil Pinder
Ashley Platt	Stacey Platt
David Platt	Dawn King-Hunter
John Paul Savill	John Savill
McKenzie Savill	Kendra Wolsey
Lorraine Wolsey	

The students and teachers at Erskine School

Special thanks to Keith McArthur of B. Macabee's Booksellers of Lethbridge, Alberta who allowed pictures to be taken in the store and whose picture appears.

Introduction

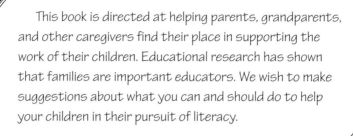

This book is directed at helping parents, grandparents, and other caregivers find their place in supporting the work of their children. Educational research has shown that families are important educators. We wish to make suggestions about what you can and should do to help your children in their pursuit of literacy.

Why This Book Was Conceived

The inspiration for the content of this book grew from conversations among friends who are educators: David, a former administrator now working as a teacher in a large urban elementary school; Robin, a university professor primarily responsible for the introduction and refinement of language learning skills of preservice teachers; and Lisa, a former elementary school teacher, now working in an alternative junior/senior high school. We are also parents of seven children who range in age from 10 months to 21 years. Over the years we have become increasingly interested in helping other parents feel both comfortable and competent as they develop ways to support their children's development as successful readers and writers.

Robin was standing in line at the supermarket check-out recently when another parent approached and questioned her about something new at school called, "three-way student-parent-teacher interviews." The parent began, "Did you learn anything about how your child was doing? What a waste of time! All we did was play a game on the computer. What I wanted to know is how my child is doing in school!" While Robin wanted to at least try to give the teacher's perspective on this form of interview, she was also a parent who had experienced some frustrations about a child's education.

Parents and teachers come together frequently over the course of twelve years of a child's education. Each group needs to understand the other's point of view in doing what is best for each child. This is why we wrote *From Your Child's Teacher: Helping Your Child Learn To Read, Write, and Speak*.

Throughout this book you will meet children and the many parents and teachers we have had the privilege to work with over the years. We experience frustration, puzzlement, joy, and laughter as we work to help children learn to read and write and to love these pursuits. In our conversations, we have learned that what we have in common with other parents is belief and hope. We believe that children are worthy and capable of succeeding at learning to read and write as well as enjoy doing it. Our hope is that some day all children will have the opportunity to develop these skills to their fullest potential.

But having belief and hope in today's society is often not enough. We need more. We need strategies and support and we need help to ensure our children develop into readers and writers so that they can meet the future with confidence, success, and joy.

Through relationships with other parents, some who are teachers but many who are not, the three of us came to realize that there is much to say about literacy and what we, as parents, can do to help our children develop successfully as readers and writers. This is not just for parents of children who are school-aged but it is also for those with infants who want to begin routines that will carry our children into elementary school, through adolescence, and throughout their lives.

Parents are a child's first and most important teachers.

Parents are a child's first and most important teachers. Among other important lessons, it is clear that home is where the foundations of literacy are laid. All homes are different but they share common characteristics that make them natural learning environments. What we mean by this is that all homes provide activities that make it possible for children to learn to speak. However, sometimes parents are not sure what those activities are.

Learning to talk is a complex task that most children accomplish without a single, formal lesson. Children succeed because certain things happen, that is, they are allowed to develop in their own way at their own pace. There is an absence of competition and testing. Parents expect that learning to talk will occur naturally. All efforts and attempts are met with enthusiasm and delight. The twelve-month-old who points to a bottle of milk and says something like, "Aaam!" is greeted with, "Yes, yes, you want some milk! Here you go. Here's your milk." Having received such positive feedback for her efforts, this baby will surely try talking again and again. Whatever the child says is accepted and praised. Moreover, in the home children are surrounded by language and receive countless demonstrations of how language works. For instance, a parent feeds his child lunch until the toddler decides it is time to feed herself. The child reaches for the spoon. The parent enthusiastically says "spoon" and hands the spoon to the child, who is delighted to get what she wanted. The parent believes his child is clever, yet this event is just one of many language lessons she will receive during the first few years of her life.

> **Learning in the first few years is self-paced and self-programmed.**

Learning in the first few years is self-paced and self-programmed. There are no set exercises or drills and practice is voluntary because children want to become members of the "talking club." Children succeed in learning to speak because of the natural environment for learning. Can learning to read and write also occur for very young children? Yes, it can. For example, when a father drives to *McDonald's* and tells his two-year-old to look for the big yellow **M**, he is teaching reading in a way that is natural and part of everyday activity.

Unfortunately, many parents are not as comfortable reading as others might be. All of us lead busy lives and we have become dependent on other forms of communication (TV or radio). Still others may be adept at reading but seldom choose to read for leisure because they do not enjoy most books or magazines. Attitudes to writing vary as well. A friend recalled a period of years when she wrote little more than birthday cards. The telephone has for the most part replaced the letter-writing tradition.

Even though few of us aspire to authorship, the written word is a key element in our daily lives. Whatever your experiences with reading and writing, one thing is certain—the foundations for literacy are laid in the early years.

There are many books on literacy development for teachers.... Resources for parents are limited.

There are many books on literacy development for teachers. If teachers want to learn about recent trends in teaching children to read with understanding, to write creatively, or to speak with confidence, then the tools are there for them. Resources for parents are limited. We have to trust the professionals (which we do) until there is a problem and then we find out what it is we could have, or perhaps should have been doing with our children all along. Parents must have information on literacy development before a problem arises. We already do many things with our children to bolster their confidence and to support them while they learn to read and write. Parents need to know that what they do at home *is* important and why.

The potential for literacy exists in every child.

The potential for literacy exists in every child. This is the spirit that drives our work. *From Your Child's Teacher* will provide parents with a family-oriented resource with information, anecdotes, ideas, activities, suggestions, and routines to build on family strengths that will enhance literacy development.

reading

and

books

"Research has shown that young children benefit in many ways from frequent activites with books. They have larger, more literate vocabularies and learn to read better than children who have had few book experiences." (McGee, 1998)

Section One: Reading and Books

Section One describes how children learn to read. It highlights the fact that no two children develop as readers in the same way. Nonetheless, there are signposts to watch for along the way and parents need to know what these are and how to respond appropriately. This section is organized according to the age and developmental levels of children to indicate how the needs and interests of readers change over time. It includes both teacher expectations and booklists as well as home activities to support and encourage reading development. For instance, one of the most important activities that can predict later reading success is "story time" where the parent reads to or with his/her child(ren). It is important to focus on this activity. We think it's also imperative to point out some of the problems and pitfalls real families face along the way. This section also includes a discussion of phonics-type games and whether they are beneficial in helping children learn to read. Finally, this section, like those that follow, features "What You May Be Concerned About" where many commonly asked questions are listed and responses are given.

Chapter One: When to Begin

There is nothing better you can do to help your child learn to read and get better at it than to read with her.

Reading is one of those fundamental things that adults either do and enjoy, or find difficult and avoid. As adults, many of us simply do not choose to read. This does not necessarily mean we cannot read or do not want to. We live busy lives. TV and radio provide up-to-date information and so reading may not be regarded as an important daily activity. However, whatever your experience with reading, there is nothing better you can do to help your child learn to read and get better at it than to read with her. Here are some strategies to follow.

Start right away.

Start right away. And start where you feel comfortable. Some parents play music and read to their children even before they are

From Your Child's Teacher

born. But even if you didn't start quite that early, don't worry. The good news is that it is never too late to begin a routine of daily reading with your child.

Make sure your home contains lots of reading material.

Make sure your home contains lots of reading material—books (your own, friends', or those from the library), magazines, and newspapers. Provide a bulletin board for notes and messages. Newsletters, photographs, cards, and letters sent from school can be displayed on the fridge.

Those of us with young children know how difficult grocery shopping can be—all that stuff just there for the taking! One way to keep children happy and encourage a love of reading is to provide a book for your toddler to look at during the shopping trip. You may want to add to your home library by choosing one of the reasonably priced selections available in most stores.

Every time you read, you are telling your child, through your actions, that reading is important.

Remember that every time you read, you are telling your child, through your actions, that reading is important. When reading a newspaper, a cookbook to learn a new recipe, or a manual on how to put together a new bicycle, reading can be a useful and enjoyable experience. These actions can go a long way in encouraging children to want to read. Not long ago, a grade four student was asked whether it would matter to him if he could not read. He thought for a moment and replied, "As long as I could read checks, it wouldn't matter." This boy's comment is a reminder that reading serves many purposes. Reading a check is not only an important ability but also it gives us great pleasure. It is clear that the value of reading was not readily apparent to this boy. Remember, it's not what you read that counts—it's that you read.

Show your children that reading is important to you

Helpful Hints for Starting Reading Routines

 Start reading to your child today.

 Make sure your home contains lots of reading material—library books, magazines, newspapers, recipe books, notes, and messages posted on a bulletin board.

 Show your child that you read.

Chapter Two: How to Read with Your Child

Birth to Two Years

Your child may have many toys during these years—teething rings, soft cuddly animals, blocks, cars, and books. Some parents begin their children on plastic-coated "bath time" books, not only because they can be played with in the tub, but also because they are virtually indestructible. There are also cloth and cardboard books for this age group. Children and babies can suck on them, chew them, throw them, and occasionally look at them. While it may seem that they are not getting much "reading" done, they are learning about books. There are interesting things to look at and one can turn pages to see new things. Parents chuckle when they see their young child staring intently at a book and sometimes babbling away while it is upside down! Cardboard books for very young children are quite popular. Many children teeth their way through their favorites. A wide variety of books are available at a reasonable cost for children under two years of age.

If you have a young child who needs to be occupied temporarily while you are making supper, then offer her a magazine or a catalogue to look at while she sits in a high chair or play pen. Many children love to turn or rip the pages and find faces to look at in this captive place.

> **As your infant grows, she will love to sit in your lap as you hold a book in front of the two of you and read aloud.**

As your infant grows, she will love to sit in your lap as you hold a book in front of the two of you and read aloud. As an activity during the day or as an evening routine, there is nothing more important you can do with or for your young child. We believe an early start to reading is invaluable for a child's future literacy development.

Visits to your local library ensure a wide variety of books are in your home.

Visits to your local library ensure a wide variety of books are in your home. Just be aware that, from time to time, a book is likely to go astray or become irreparably damaged. Amy, Robin's oldest daughter, colored an entire library book orange one day. Rather than return the "new" version of the book, they paid for it and kept it. Amy, now older, still chuckles that she could ever have committed such an act.

Your own personal photograph albums are sources of enjoyment and "reading" for you and your child.

Your own personal photograph albums are sources of enjoyment and "reading" for you and your child. Children enjoy viewing photos of themselves and family members. As you point to pictures, talk to your child about what you are viewing: "There's a picture of Auntie Emma. Look, she's eating some birthday cake!"

Helpful Hints: Birth to Two Years

 Sit comfortably with your child in your lap while you hold a book, read aloud, and talk about the pictures.

 Offer your baby a magazine to look at in her high chair or play pen while you cook supper.

 Visit your local library to ensure a wide variety of books are in your home.

 Look at photograph albums with your child and tell the story of the events shown in the photos.

Ages Three to Six

Toddlers and preschoolers seem to thrive on routines that have been introduced and practiced since birth. Have you tried to skip a part in a favorite storybook hoping to move things along only to have your sleepy child protest loudly that that is not how the story goes? In the evening, after teeth are brushed and the TV is turned off, we read for fifteen to thirty minutes before bedtime. Such a routine already begun before a child begins school will be enormously helpful when homework begins.

Allow your children to choose some library books for themselves as they begin to develop interests and preferences of their own.

Allow your children to choose some library books for themselves as they begin to develop interests and preferences of their own, even if some choices seem too easy or too hard. This helps later on when the older child examines an entire school library of books and cries, "I can't find anything I like!" Of course, you can pick books you'd like to read to your child, too. Be sure to read both storybooks as well as information books. Some children who don't seem to like reading will come alive when faced with a book of photographs showing large machinery at work on a construction site. You can use a game called "I Pick, You Pick." The child chooses a book he or she likes and so does the parent. In this way, you can introduce new kinds of books while still letting your child make choices. Chances are, if you read something that really appeals to you, your own enthusiasm and interest will rub off on your child. That is, if you like science fiction, find similar kinds of books for a younger audience and read/enjoy these together.

Pop-up books are especially appealing to children of all ages. As these can be expensive, you might want to save these for times when you and your child are reading together.

Pop-up books are appealing

Children of this age enjoy hearing the same story over and over.

Children of this age enjoy hearing the same story over and over. This drives Lisa's husband crazy and she can sometimes hear him trying to change their daughter's mind about a book. "How about his one?... Well, we just read that one last night.... Are you sure?... Okay!" A friend tells of a time she found her son's favorite book, *Danny the Dinosaur*, in the garbage. Her son had not tired of his favorite story, but his Dad had. Even though it may sometimes be frustrating, you really are doing your child a favor by re-reading favorite stories. Your child is learning that stories are predictable. He can predict what will happen next particularly when the story is familiar. This is essential when he begins to read on his own.

Memorization and successful prediction are two important elements in learning to read.

One of the most rewarding moments of parenthood came when Robin's five-year-old daughter told her she knew her book, *Berenstain Bears Junk Food*, so well that she could read it without even opening it. David recalls his daughter, Stacey, then three years old, asking her Dad to read her favorite story, *Golly Gump* every night for six months. These are examples showing that memorization and successful prediction are two important elements in learning to read. A child who has been read to on a regular basis knows what reading is supposed to be about. Children are more successful at sounding out words and recognizing sight words if they already have a sense of story. You might be thinking, "Wait a minute, my child isn't really reading the words. She's memorized it." Precisely! For that child, memorization is the beginning of learning to read. She masters that skill and later looks more closely at the print.

Your job is to support your "memorizing" child.

Support your memorizing child

Your job is to support your "memorizing" child. When she finishes the book, say something like "Wow, that was terrific! You really know that story. Let's go back and see if we can find all the words that begin like your name—Brianne." Then, together look for words beginning with the letter **b**. This time help your child to focus on specific words that she thinks she can read.

A reading game that works well with older children is "I Start,

You Finish." The parent begins the sentence and then stops; the child continues. Once your child understands that you are looking at the print (letters, words, and sentences) on a page when you read, begin doing something called tracking. Point to the words as you read them to show your child that the words you are saying correspond to the print. This is helpful for children who are just beginning to read. At this stage try to choose storybooks with only a few sentences on each page. As children choose books with more sentences on each page to read, you may find it helpful to encourage them to follow the print. Tracking helps a child keep her place while reading. Once a child begins to read well, however, tracking actually slows her down.

Finally, when reading with your child, do not worry if you do not have a radio-type voice or if you are self-conscious about using other voices during story time. Your child enjoys the time spent reading because she is with you. Whether you are a boisterous, dramatic reader or a quiet, peaceful reader, your child still benefits from the time spent together reading. Interestingly, we have found that we improve as oral readers by reading often to our children. However, try not to have the same adult read all the time. Let your spouse or a grandparent read to your children to avoid the situation a friend of ours found herself in. She always read the bedtime stories to her children. One evening, she had to be out and was not able to read. She explained, "Tonight, Daddy will read you a story!" Her children looked at her suspiciously. "Can Daddy read?" they asked.

Helpful Hints: Ages Three to Six

 When your child finishes "reading" a page say, "Wow, that was terrific! You really know that story. Let's go back and see if we can find all the words that begin like your name—Brianne."

 Try a reading game called, "I Start, You Finish." The parent begins the sentence or paragraph and then stops; the child continues.

 Use tracking by pointing to the words as you read them to show your child that the words you are saying are the words on the page. Eventually, your child will take over this task.

Ages Seven to Ten

Your child is now at school and will be expected to read what the teacher presents. These may be readers, textbooks, library books, charts, and individually made booklets. Whatever your child's teacher uses for instruction, it is important to continue reading at home. You may wish to encourage your child to do more of the reading since practice is needed. This should not, however, replace your reading to your child.

Reading library books at home

One method is the "My Turn, Your Turn" type of shared reading. You might read one page or one book and then have your child read one. If this proves too overwhelming, try reading one page or one line and then have your child do the same. Another way to encourage your child to read is the "Fade In, Fade Out" method. In this way, you and your child begin reading the book aloud together. As you hear your child's voice getting stronger, fade out by lowering your voice. If your child struggles, then fade in again providing help until he is reading confidently again.

Feel free to ask your child questions while you are reading. Try to ensure the questions don't become more important than the story. It's a good idea to ask a child what he thinks is going to happen next. To predict successfully, he has to think about what has already happened and use logic to figure out upcoming events. Questions that help children to think about stories include:

- How are you like the character in this story?
- What would you do if you were in the story?
- Have you ever thought about doing _____?
- What kind of adventure would you like to go on?
- What does this story remind you of?

Avoid questions that *don't* get children to think about what has been read. For instance, those having "yes" or "no" answers or those whose answers are obvious, such as:

- Do you like this story?
- Is she going outside?

Another way to encourage discussion is through lead-ins. The parent says things like, "I really liked the part _____," and lets her child finish the phrase. Or say, "One thing I am wondering about this story is _____" and wait for your child to say something.

Ages Eleven and Up

A child's interest in a topic often motivates her to read.

At this stage, your child will read more and more for school. She is probably reading books for language arts as well as in the areas of mathematics, social studies, science, and others. Your role may be to ask her about her reading in these areas. Is she finding words, passages, ideas, or concepts difficult? If so, ask the teacher about having copies of school textbooks at home. Another way to help your child as she begins reading in other subjects is to choose library books that help her understand a new area. For example, a picture book about the human body will not only be interesting but will also help your child learn about things related to the school subjects of health

Reading as a family activity at all ages

and physical education. Many parents find that children have a natural interest in dinosaurs. With just a few books, it is amazing how children learn to read and pronounce difficult words like **Stegosaurus**, **Tyrannosaurus Rex**, and **Triceratops**. Yet shorter words such as **this**, **house**, and **dog** are stumbling blocks. A child's interest in a topic often motivates her to read.

Be sure to keep reading to your child. Share a new story from the newspaper, a recipe you like, or an excerpt from a book you are reading. Whatever the source, show your older child that reading is an important part of your life. Ask your child what she is reading to show your interest.

Reading is a lifelong process.

Reading is a lifelong process. If we show our children that reading is important to us by making time for it every day (or nearly every day), then they will learn to read successfully and apply it in everything they do.

Helpful Hints: Ages Eleven and Up

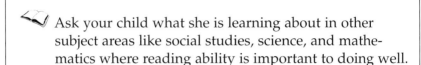 Ask your child what she is learning about in other subject areas like social studies, science, and mathematics where reading ability is important to doing well.

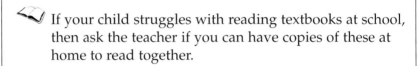 If your child struggles with reading textbooks at school, then ask the teacher if you can have copies of these at home to read together.

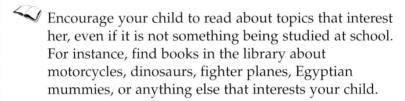 Encourage your child to read about topics that interest her, even if it is not something being studied at school. For instance, find books in the library about motorcycles, dinosaurs, fighter planes, Egyptian mummies, or anything else that interests your child.

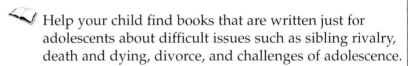 Help your child find books that are written just for adolescents about difficult issues such as sibling rivalry, death and dying, divorce, and challenges of adolescence.

Helping the School-Age Child

Once in school many children bring home books on a weekly basis from the school library. In most cases the class signs out books on the same day each week and returns them a week later. If you share books regularly with your child up until this point, one book a week isn't going to be enough. It is important to continue your trips to the public library. Try reading the occasional chapter book, one, two or more chapters a night. Lists of chapter books appropriate for different ages are included at the end of this section and in the final section.

At some point, your child will likely begin to read independently. Parents often cease to make reading to their children a priority when they are able to read on their own.

However, they are still developing as readers and continue to need models of good reading. Children are able to understand books that are too difficult for them to read independently so your role as reader is still important. Recently when Robin was reading to her eight-year-old, they were interrupted by the baby crying. Robin stopped reading and said she would be back to continue once she had attended to the baby. When she returned, Amy was reading the next part aloud and was halfway through the next chapter. The story was interesting enough to Amy to keep reading. Of course, then Robin had to catch up!

Another lesson learned. Some parents take turns reading to their children from week to week rather than from night to night. They found they were frustrated by reading only every other chapter in a book when taking turns reading. The children heard the whole story but the parents didn't! Good modeling also occurs when everyone sits down and reads silently together. That way, each family member can enjoy his or her own reading material.

Talking Together

If your child likes to curl up with a book, interrupt from time to time and ask your child about what she has read. You find out if she really understands what is happening in the book. It is important to keep this as relaxed and nonthreatening as possible. Use questions or comments like, "What do you think will happen next?" or "Can you picture in your mind what the cabin looks like?" or "That character seems _____."(Wait for your child to respond.)

Curling up with a book

Robin experienced a similar situation not too long ago. While reading a story called *Something New* to her daughter Amy, she noticed (though not at first) that the illustrator used black and white pictures to show action in England and color pictures to show what was happening at the same time in Canada. She asked her daughter if she could guess why some pictures were in color while others were in black and white. She could not, so Robin explained that the black and white pictures were used to show England during wartime when life was hard and people didn't have much, and the color pictures showed Canada where the war was less of a hardship. When Amy took the book to school the next day, she shared the information with her teacher and friends who were not able to guess why the illustrator used such an interesting style.

Illustrations

Children and adults enjoy certain books because of the interesting illustrations.

Children and adults enjoy certain books because of the interesting illustrations. Barbara Reid's illustrations capture children's attention because they are created from Plasticine. Phoebe Gilman's art is colorful and lifelike. For books like these, it is natural for children to focus their attention more on the pictures than on the words. Children who interrupt your reading to talk about the pictures are showing they understand that print and pictures go together to tell a story. It can be frustrating, but try to talk about things that interest your child in a particular book. Another way to handle this is to go through the book the first time with your child by just looking at the pictures and talking about what is being illustrated.

Children of this age often develop strong likes and dislikes for certain books, authors, or topics. Many six- and seven-year-olds adore Robert Munsch books. You may find yourself reading these several hundred times before they are retired temporarily. The same may be true once children find a book series they like—the Bailey School Kids series, Nancy Drew/Hardy Boys series, Goosebumps series, the Ramona books, Babysitter's Club, or *Archie* comic books. Though it is important to let children make their own choices, try to supplement these with other books that you choose. If young

Talking about illustrations

children learn to choose their own books, on topics they love, they will be more interested in reading! But if a book is going nowhere, you don't like it, your child doesn't like it—leave it. Do not force the issue. Some children can be turned off reading altogether with too many experiences like this.

Other Helpful Hints About Reading to Children

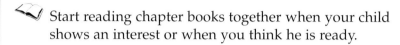 Start reading chapter books together when your child shows an interest or when you think he is ready.

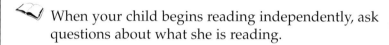 When your child begins reading independently, ask questions about what she is reading.

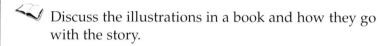 Discuss the illustrations in a book and how they go with the story.

 Choose books for your child, but also allow him to choose many of the books he reads.

Chapter Three: How Children Learn to Read

Learning to read is like a miracle when we observe the process in our own children.

Learning to read is like a miracle when we observe the process in our own children. One day they are content to listen to every word we read and the next day they are reading the words to us. Every child learns to read in his own way. If you are a parent of more than one school-aged child, you already know this. Your first child may have struggled to learn to read, only reading with ease at the end of grade two. The younger child, however picked up the older sibling's books and began reading before entering grade one. Parents often scratch their heads in wonder, thinking that both children should have learned to read in exactly the same way. Why didn't they develop as readers in the same way? The answer is that they are two different people.

Some Common Ways Children Learn to Read

Some of the more common ways children learn to read are:

1. **Sight Words.** Some children memorize many of the words they see and hear often. Words become known to them through repetition. Children usually learn to recognize their own names and the names of brothers, sisters, and friends as sight words. Other words are also learned this way, such as **stop, McDonald's, milk,** or **Crest**. These words are learned easily because of their recognizable color, shape, and size. Because children see these words so often in their homes, in neighborhoods, and in grocery stores, they recognize them quickly and easily. In most cases, children who teach themselves to read before entering school do so with the sight word method, using their ability to memorize new words based on how those words look.

2. **Phonics.** This method is probably the best known to parents who remember learning to read this way. Many children learn to read by sounding out words. They learn from parents, siblings, and teachers that letters have both names and sounds. For example, the letter **m** makes the **m/m/m** sound at the beginning and end of **mom**. This method is helpful for many words—**cat, lift, sand, stop**. It can be confusing, however, for other words such as **does, there, laugh,** and **school**.

Nevertheless, it is important for all children to know how to sound out words even if they do not always use this method.

Some children learn to write before they learn to read although most learn these skills at the same time.

Some children learn to write before they learn to read although most learn these skills at the same time. Often they do so because they have an interest in letters and their sounds and they want to express themselves. These children begin by writing everything phonetically. For instance, **I lik mi mom** would be read as **I like my mom**. These children often develop successfully as readers when they turn their attention to reading because they have already figured out how some words are put together.

3. **Making Sense.** Usually children who learn to read by "making sense" also use one or both of the first two methods. They may be reading along when an unfamiliar word appears. The word might be **strange**. The child may try to sound it out without success, so he may try one of the following. He may look more closely at the picture for a clue to help with the word. He may continue reading to see if what follows helps him to make sense of the unknown word. In other words, the child is trying to make sense of the story and to decode the word. He does this by figuring out if the word fits with the story, that is, using context clues to figure out unfamiliar words. It is clear that children who have some idea of letter sounds also use that knowledge to help them make sense of unfamiliar words. It is much like an adult trying to solve a problem. When one solution does not work, he tries something else.

4. **Memorization.** As previously mentioned, some children memorize favorite stories. Parents are often amazed at a child's ability to retell a particularly long or complicated story word for word. Sometimes they memorize a chorus or often-repeated phrase from a story. An example of an often favorite refrain is from Bill Martin Jr.'s *Chicka Chicka, ABC*. It goes like this, "Chicka, chicka, boom, boom. Will there be enough room at the top of the coconut tree?" These children may or may not actually look at the words they are "reading" and they may or may not think that they are reading. However, for some children, this method is essential to getting them started on reading.

reading and books

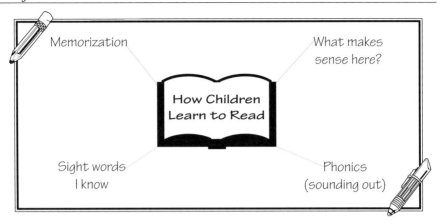

Successful readers use a combination of two or more of these methods when learning to read. If one method doesn't work, then they have another to try. As a result, giving up occurs far less. As parents, it is helpful to our children to show them more than one method for making sense of words and sentences. You can provide help in the following ways.

Stuck on a Word? Steps to Help Your Child

If your child is reading to you and comes to an unfamiliar word:

1. Wait three or four seconds to see what she does. If this doesn't work, then go on to the next step.

2. Say, "Can you sound out the word?" Make the first sound(s) to get him started. If this doesn't work, then go on to the next step.

3. If she sounds out each letter but still doesn't know what the word is, then suggest she look at the picture. Does this help? If this doesn't work, then go on to the next step.

4. Read the sentence again and stop before the unfamiliar word. Does this help? If this doesn't work, then go on to the next step.

5. Skip that word and have the child continue reading. Does he figure it out by reading to the end of the sentence, paragraph, or page?

Your child will likely make sense of the new word during this short session. If not, simply tell her the word, saying, for example, "**action** is a difficult word because it has the letters **tion** that we read as **shun**." Then go on. Depending on your child's interest level, you could discuss other similar words as well.

Learning to Read—A Lesson for Adults

Imagine that you have just been given a book to read. It is a book on a topic about which you know absolutely nothing. This may be a physics textbook or a technical manual. The task is to make sense of this book. How do you begin?

First, leaf through the book as you would do with a magazine in a grocery check-out line. When you come to a page that catches your eye, stop and examine it, maybe read a caption or title, and continue on. Look at the title of the book and maybe the name of the author to see if there is something you recognize. Look at the Table of Contents. Does a certain chapter title sound familiar or interesting? If there is a chapter that you want to examine, then locate the page number in the Table of Contents and find it in the book. Look through the chapter for pictures, diagrams, words in bold-faced type, and other familiar kinds of information. Read parts of the chapter to see if you can make sense of it. When you come to a word you do not know, sound it out, skip over it, or come back to it after having finished reading the sentence. You will likely read more slowly than if you were reading a magazine. At some point, you may become completely frustrated and close the book altogether! What you have just done is what young children often do when they are first learning to read.

From this short description, you can see that reading involves many different behaviors. Note that sounding out words or phonics was just one of the methods you used to try to understand the text. The same is true for young children who are just learning to read. They do need to know about phonics letters which are connected with certain sounds to sound out some of the words they read. But it's important to remember all those other things we do when reading something that is difficult for us to understand.

Kids Are Smart

In school and at home, children need to learn many behaviors to help them with reading. Young children who have been read to on a daily basis before coming to school and who pick up books and "pretend" to read, know some things about reading that will make learning to read much easier. They know that the cover tells the title and the author. They know when a book is upside-down. They know how to turn the pages from beginning to end. They know that the pictures are an important part of the story and they may even know some of the words because they have seen and heard them over and over again. In other words, these children are doing the same kinds of things you did with the physics book.

Understanding "reading"

Remember when you found a word you didn't know in the physics book? What did you do? You sounded it out. Notice that "sounding-out" was only one of the ways you tried to understand the content of the book. It is important to teach a variety of reading strategies to children. So, if your child is reading and comes to an unfamiliar word, then try saying, "Let's sound it out." Make the sounds with your child. Or ask the child to read from the beginning of the sentence and see what word would make sense in that spot. Or have your child skip over the word and read to the end of the sentence before asking what the word might be. Give your child at least four seconds to make sense of the word on her own before reading it aloud. If you use some of these ideas, then you will be helping your child use many ways to decode new words. One method is not enough to help children with the many words they will find in their reading. Use the strategies listed above and show your child there are lots of ways to figure out words! These problem-solving strategies will make reading more enjoyable and lead to lifelong learning.

The Scoop on Phonics Games and Books

Not long ago Robin was speaking to a group of parents about reading to young children before they come to school. Robin explained that the act of reading to a child prior to schooling has been shown to be an effective way to encourage the child's own success as a reader. One parent offered that she spent lots of time reading to her children and then indicated that she had also invested in an expensive phonics game for her two- and four-year-old. She wanted to know what we thought about such games and activities.

Phonics games, books, and activities often force a child to focus on letters and sounds. This is not necessarily a bad thing, however, you can do similar activities without investing a lot of money. For example, if you make a habit of pointing out letters on signs, advertising, and stores, then you accomplish the same thing. Simply by saying, "There's a stop sign; it starts like this—ssssss," you have just given your child a lesson in phonics. With discarded magazines and catalogues, you and your child can make a collage of pictures of things that begin with a certain letter of the alphabet. Displaying the collage on the refrigerator then helps your child to remember the letters you are practicing.

Interestingly, after Robin finished speaking to the group, she asked the parent, who had spent $300 on the phonics game, "Now that you know more about how children learn to read and how the phonics game works, do you think you could have accomplished the same goals using simple, less expensive materials around the house and around the community?" The parent replied, "Absolutely!"

Many researchers agree that phonics games and workbooks used without the context of real stories tend to be meaningless to young children. Meguido Zola from Simon Fraser University tells us that in order for children to understand why phonics skills are learned, they need to stay away from "drill and skill" activities such as expensive packages of phonics materials that have no real connection to learning to read. Instead, it is suggested that parents read books of nursery rhymes and children's poetry to interest children in how language sounds. Authors who write in this genre are Sheree Fitch, Dennis Lee, and Shel Silverstein to name only a few. Sharing storybooks about the alphabet is another way to help children understand how language works. Books such as, *Anamalia* by Graeme Base and *The Alphabet from Z to A: With Much Confusion on the Way* by Judith Viorst, help children to connect with letters and sounds in a way that makes sense and is fun.

Many other books of these types are listed in the book lists of Section Five of this book to help parents select books to read with their children. Another excellent source of information on books for children is the children's librarian at the local library. She or he can help parents find books suitable for any age or interest.

The Ways Readers Understand Print

 Sight Words. These are words that become known through repetition. They include children's own names, stop and yield signs, and store signs.

 Phonics. This a method where children are taught to sound out a word by saying the sound of each individual letter.

 Making Sense. This is where children use pictures and/or the rest of a sentence to help them figure out an unknown word.

 Memorization. This is when children retell a story, sometimes word for word, because they have heard it often and have committed it to memory.

Chapter Four: What the Teacher Does and Why

> As parents and teachers ourselves, we also want what is best for our children. However, what is best for one child may or may not be best for another child.

Over the past decade, public interest in how children learn to read and write has grown. Parents have questions about how their children are being taught to read and write. More and more, parents ask if they should buy a specific home-reading program for their preschooler who is not yet showing an interest in reading. They want to know if their child's teacher is spending too much or too little time on spelling. These parents may think there is one best and correct way to teach reading and, of course, they want the teacher to use that method. As parents and teachers ourselves, we also want what is best for our children. However, what is best for one child may or may not be best for another child. It is only through direct observation of children in the process of everyday reading that teachers can make decisions about how best to support literacy development in individual children. It might be helpful to look at how teaching reading has changed over the past thirty years.

What Teachers Used to Do

Teachers were taught to teach reading by breaking language down into its smallest parts, starting first with letter names and sounds and then combining these to produce short words that could easily be sounded out like—**cat, Sam, am, fast**. Eventually, these words were combined into sentences that were easy to sound out but that didn't make much story sense to young children—"Nat sat on a mat." Usually, there was one sentence on a page combined with a simple picture. Remember the Dick and Jane books? "See Jane. See Jane run. Run Jane, run." Such books, while achieving a purpose, did not captivate or motivate the young reader. Consequently, many children found learning to read a struggle. Critics of this instructional approach suggested that the teaching of reading didn't make sense to young children. They also suggested that beginning reading should start with whole stories that are both interesting and fun.

What Teachers Do Now

More and more teachers are encouraged to begin teaching reading by sharing whole stories with children. This is done to help children get a sense of story—knowing there is a beginning, a middle, and an ending. Once children know that reading means the sharing of a story and the turning of pages, the teacher is then encouraged to break language down into words and sounds for children to recognize and learn.

Sharing stories

Both of these methods have the same goal—teaching children to read successfully. The major difference between them is how and when to teach specific reading skills like sounding out letters and words. The diagrams on the next page show how these two teaching methods differ. Notice that both approaches teach the same skills; it is the order in which they are taught that varies.

What You Might See in Your Child's Classroom

Learning to read should be child-centered. It is important to place the child in environments at home and at school where reading is viewed as an interesting, purposeful, and natural activity. Reading different kinds of stories to children helps them understand what reading is for. It is for enjoyment, for laughter, for learning, and for communicating. While reading, skills like sounding out unfamiliar words can be introduced, practiced, and refined. Teachers use worksheets and tests to see whether children are acquiring reading skills. However, it is important that children see and understand how these skill activities relate to overall reading enjoyment. It is our belief that such skill activities enhance and reinforce the purpose for reading and should not be the main focus of a reading lesson.

reading and books

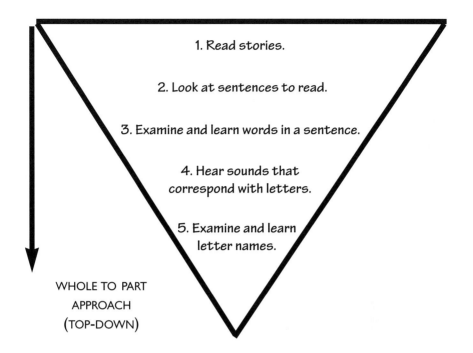

WHOLE TO PART
APPROACH
(TOP-DOWN)

1. Read stories.
2. Look at sentences to read.
3. Examine and learn words in a sentence.
4. Hear sounds that correspond with letters.
5. Examine and learn letter names.

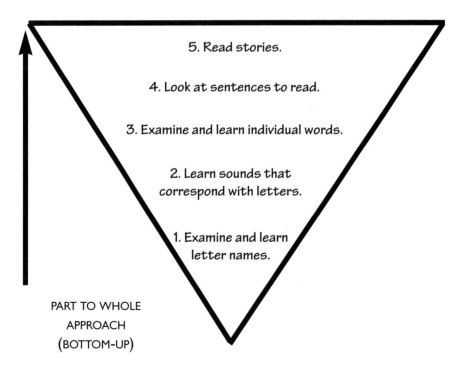

PART TO WHOLE
APPROACH
(BOTTOM-UP)

5. Read stories.
4. Look at sentences to read.
3. Examine and learn individual words.
2. Learn sounds that correspond with letters.
1. Examine and learn letter names.

reading and books

In many elementary classrooms, teachers help children choose and enjoy books and then teach skills in one or more of the following ways:

1. They help children sound out words by teaching sounds and letters or combinations of sounds.
2. They define words or help children put into their own words the meanings of new vocabulary words.
3. They talk about how the illustrations in a story go with the words and ideas on the page.
4. They have children talk or write about the beginning, middle, and end of a story.
5. They show that we read from left to right by using their fingers to track across a page.
6. They demonstrate how punctuation is used in reading.
7. They model good oral reading by reading with expression.
8. They encourage children to read independently, with partners of various ages and in small groups to help build confidence in reading.
9. They copy out parts of stories or whole stories onto chart paper so that children can chant stories orally together or individually.
10. They send books home so children will keep reading at home and practice a particular story to share at school.
11. They talk about favorite authors and illustrators with children so that they learn who writes books and how books are put together.
12. They help children to use many ways to figure out new words—sounding out, making sense, rereading a sentence, finishing the sentence and then going back, or getting help from a friend or teacher.

As a parent, you may use some of these strategies with your children. Teaching a child to read and learn specific reading skills will always be achieved through reading with and for a more experienced reader (the teacher, parent, guardian, older sibling).

It is important to remember that reading progress is not determined by how many books you go through in an evening or a month but by the interest your child shows in reading and the variety of stories your child can read.

It is important to remember that reading progress is not determined by how many books you go through in an evening or a month but by the interest your child shows in reading and the variety of stories your child can read. It is true that children will return to favorite books from time to time. Teachers encourage this type of rereading but they also encourage children to select books that introduce more difficult words and more complex story lines. All types of reading skills may be fostered at school and at home. Yet every child presents a unique challenge to the teacher who must find the best way to encourage learning to read, based upon what that child needs as a beginning reader and what his skills are. Always, it is expected that children will learn skills such as phonics, vocabulary development, comprehension, and inference through real reading activities.

Some Terms Teachers Use

Phonics—This a method where children are taught to sound out a word by saying the sound of each individual letter.

Vocabulary Development—Through reading, children learn the meanings of new words. The teacher may have children use these new words in the sentences and stories they write.

Comprehension—This refers to a child's ability to retell parts of, or entire stories they have read. They must be able to show that they have understood a passage or a story.

Inference—In stories and books, authors do not often state exactly what has happened. It is the reader's job to figure it out by "reading between the lines," that is, by inferring what has happened. This skill is developed by reading and talking about stories.

Chapter Five: What to Read

Birth to Two Years

> **The books you share with your baby or toddler should be sturdy!**

The books you share with your baby or toddler should be sturdy! Choose plastic "bath" books, cardboard books, or cloth books. As children progress, they will enjoy pop-up books. The following list can be used to guide your choices. (Additional books at each level are listed in Section Five.)

BOOK LIST FOR BIRTH TO TWO YEARS

Apple, Margot. (1990). *Blanket*. Boston: Houghton.

Arnold, Tedd. (1987). *No Jumping on the Bed!* [illus by author]. New York: Dial.

Brown, Margaret Wise. (1947). *Goodnight Moon* [illus by Clement Hurd]. New York: Harper.

Carle, Eric. (1971). *Do You Want to Be My Friend?* [illus by author]. New York: Harper.

Chorao, Kay. (1986). *The Baby's Good Morning Book* [illus by author]. New York: Dutton.

Hale, Sara Josepha. (1990). *Mary Had a Little Lamb* [illus by Bruce McMillan]. New York: Scholastic.

Hill, Eric. (1989). *Spot Counts from 1 to 10* [illus by author]. [Series: Little Spot Board Books] New York: Putnam.

Jackson, Ellen. (1991). *Ants Can't Dance* [illus by Frank Remkiewicz]. New York: Macmillan.

Jonas, Ann. (1984). *Holes and Peeks* [illus by author]. New York: Greenwillow.

Mayer, Mercer. (1987). *There's an Alligator Under My Bed* [illus by author]. New York: Dial.

Mother Goose. (1993). *The House That Jack Built* [illus by Emily Bolam]. New York: Dutton.

Oxenbury, Helen. (1987). *Clap Hands*. New York: Macmillan.

Oxenbury, Helen. (1987). *Say Goodnight* [illus by author]. New York: Macmillan.

Reid, Barbara. (1991). *Zoe's Rainy Day* [illus by author]. Toronto, ON: Harper Collins.

Stinson, Cathy. (1982.) *Red is Best.* Toronto, ON: Annick.

Ages Three to Six

As children develop, they may begin to read by themselves or retell favorite stories, using their own words or by memorizing parts of stories or whole stories.

Most children this age love to sit close to you as you read to them. The books listed here represent a range of stories from picture books (with no words) to elaborate story lines; from repetitive stories to information books; from alphabet and number books to silly tongue-twisting poetry. You and your child will certainly have your own favorites!

As children develop, they may begin to read by themselves or retell favorite stories, using their own words or by memorizing parts of stories or whole stories. Many of the books listed here encourage children to role play reading on their own. However, you will find that other books we have suggested can only be read by an older reader and are meant to be shared with a younger child.

Some books have colorful and interesting illustrations that often appeal to young children. These books encourage children to really look at the pictures to find out as much as they can.

The following book list may be useful to you as your child gets older, too.

Ages three to six

This is because seven- to ten-year-olds may use books on *this* list when they begin to read on their own. David's children received the book, *The Polar Express* by Chris Van Allsberg when they were not yet school-age, yet they loved the story and its illustrations. The book contains difficult content, understood more by adults than by children, but it is appealing to young children when read to them.

BOOK LIST FOR AGES THREE TO SIX

Anno, Mitsumasa. (1995). *Anno's Magic Seeds.* New York: Putnam/Philomel.

Carle, Eric. (1981). *The Very Hungry Caterpillar* [illus by author]. New York: Putnam.

Crews, Donald. (1994). *Sail Away* [illus]. New York: Greenwillow.

Edwards, Frank B. (1995). *Mortimer Mooner Makes Lunch* [illus by John Bianchi]. Kingston, ON: Bungalo Books.

Ehlert, Lois. (1992). *Nuts to You* [illus]. San Diego: Harcourt.

Emberley, Barbara. (1972). *Drummer Hoff* [illus by Ed Emberley]. Richmond Hill, ON: Distican.

Gilman, Phoebe. (1995). *The Gypsy Princess.* Toronto, ON: Scholastic.

Hutchins, Pat. (1985). *The Very Worst Monster* [illus by author]. New York: Greenwillow.

Hutchins, Pat. (1968). *Rosie's Walk* [illus]. New York: Simon & Schuster.

Lobel, Arnold. (1973). *Frog and Toad are Friends* [illus]. New York: Harper Collins.

Lionni, Leo. (1994). *The Mixed-Up Chameleon* [illus by author]. New York: Greenwillow.

Martin, Jr., Bill. (1992). *Brown Bear, Brown Bear, What Do You See?* (25th Anniversary Edition) [illus by Eric Carle]. New York: Henry Holt.

Mayer, Mercer. (1975). *Just For You* [illus by author]. Racine, WI: Western.

Mollel, Tololwa M. (1992). *Rhinos for Lunch and Elephants for Supper* [illus by Barbara Sprull]. Boston: Houghton Mifflin.

Munsch, Robert. (1993). *Wait and* See [illus by Michael Martchenko]. Toronto, ON: Annick.

Sendak, Maurice. (1963). *Where the Wild Things Are* [illus by author]. New York: Harper.

Trivizas, Eugene. (1994). *The Three Little Wolves and the Big Bad Pig* [illus by Helen Oxenbury]. New York: Margaret K. McElderry Books.

Van Allsburg, Chris. (1990). *Polar Express* [illus]. Boston: Houghton Mifflin.

Ward, Heather P. (1994). *I Promise I'll Find You* [illus by Sheila McGraw]. Willowdale, ON: Firefly.

Westcott, Nadine Bernard. (1980). *I Know an Old Lady Who Swallowed a Fly* [illus by author]. Boston: Little, Brown.

Ages Seven to Ten

The book list for ages three to six will still be useful with this age group. Use the following list in addition to the previous one.

Books with pictures should not be replaced by chapter books.

In our experience, many parents are convinced their children should be reading simple chapter books by grade three. This may or may not be the case. It depends on the child. Suzanne, Lisa's daughter, can and will read more difficult books but prefers picture books when choosing her own reading. However, parents can begin reading short novels aloud to introduce their children to these kinds of books. Several good examples of these are listed below.

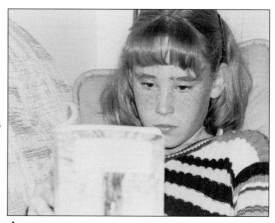

Ages seven to ten

Remember also that books with pictures should not be replaced by chapter books.

BOOK LIST FOR AGES SEVEN TO TEN

Bunting, Eve. (1989). *The Wednesday Surprise.* New York: Houghton Mifflin.

Clearly, Beverly. (1975). *Ramona the Brave.* New York: Dell.

Cooney, Barbara. (1982). *Miss Rumphius* [illus by author]. New York: Penguin.

Dahl, Roald. (1961). *James and the Giant Peach* [illus by Nancy E. Burket]. New York: Knopf.

Dorris, Michael. (1992). *Morning Girl*. New York: Hyperion.

Fitzhugh, Louise. (1964). *Harriet the Spy* [illus by author]. New York: Harper Collins.

Gilman, Phoebe. (1994). *The Lost Children* [illus by author]. New York: Bradbury.

Gilman, Phoebe. (1993). *Something From Nothing*. Toronto, ON: Scholastic.

Hoban, Lillian. (1985). *Arthur's Loose Tooth* [illus by author]. New York: Harper and Row.

Lee, Dennis. (1974). *Alligator Pie* [illus by Frank Neufeld]. Toronto, ON: Macmillan.

Lowry, Lois. (1989). *Number the Stars*. Boston: Houghton Mifflin.

McGugan, Jim. (1994). *A Prairie Boy's Story* [illus by Murray Kimber]. Red Deer, AB: Red Deer College Press.

Mollel, Tololwa M. (1991). *Orphan Boy* [illus by Paul Morin]. New York: Houghton Mifflin.

Park, Barbara. (1992). *Junie B. Jones and the Stupid Smelly School Bus* [illus by Denise Brunkus]. New York: Random House.

Scieszka, Jon. (1995). *Math Curse* [illus by Lane Smith]. New York: Viking.

Smucker, Barbara. (1995). *Selina and the Bear Paw Quilt* [illus by Janet Wilson]. Toronto, ON: Lester.

Steig, William. (1982). *Doctor De Soto*. New York: Harper Collins.

Wilder, Laura Ingalls. (1953). *Little House in the Big Woods* [illus by Garth Williams]. New York: Harper.

Yolen, Jane. (1972). *The Girl Who Loved the Wind* [illus by Ed Young]. New York: Harper Collins.

Zolotow, Charlotte. (1963). *The Quarreling Book* [illus by Arnold Lobel]. New York: Harper Collins.

Ages Eleven and Up

By this time, most children are able to read chapter books on their own. Even though your child may be reading on her own, it is still important to share books together. It can be fun to read the same book and talk about events and characters. Or try reading a book to your child that requires a higher reading level. Children can understand more difficult books that are read to them than they could understand on their own. For example, you could choose to read some classic titles that children do not normally choose for themselves, such as *Huck Finn* or *Treasure Island*. These kinds of activities establish a love of reading that will continue throughout your child's life.

Ages 11+

BOOK LIST FOR AGES ELEVEN AND UP

Avi. (1996). *Beyond the Western Sea, Book One. The Escape from Home.* New York: Orchard.

Babbit, Natalie. (1975). *Tuck Everlasting.* New York: Farrar, Straus & Giroux.

Byars, Betsy. (1992). *Coast to Coast* [illus]. New York: Dell.

Creech, Sharon. (1994). *Walk Two Moons.* New York: Harper Collins.

Cushman, Karen. (1995). *The Midwife's Apprentice.* Boston: Houghton Mifflin.

Danakas, John. (1995). *Lizzie's Soccer Showdown.* Toronto, ON: James Lorimer.

Fox, Paula. (1984). *The One-Eyed Cat* [illus by Irene Trivas]. New York: Simon & Schuster.

Godfrey, Martyn. (1984). *Here She Is Ms. Teeny Wonderful.* Richmond Hill, ON: Scholastic.

Halvorson, Marilyn. (1986). *Cowboys Don't Cry.* New York: Dell.

Hughes, Monica. (1992). *Crystal Drop.* Toronto, ON: Harper Collins.

Little, Jane. (1985). *Mama's Going to Buy You a Mockingbird.* Toronto, ON: Penguin.

Lowry, Lois. (1994). *The Giver.* Boston: Houghton Mifflin.

Montgomery, Lucy Maud. (1995). *Anne of Green Gables.* Toronto, ON: Ryerson Press.

Nayor, Phyllis Reynolds. (1991). *Shiloh.* New York: Simon & Schuster.

Paterson, Katherine. (1996). *Lyddie.* New York: Dutton.

Paterson, Katherine. (1977). *Bridge to Terabithia* [illus by Donna Diamond]. Toronto, ON: Harper Collins.

Paulsen, Gary. (1989). *Hatchet.* New York: Penguin.

Spinelli, Jerry. (1996). *Another Way to Dance.* New York: Delacorte.

Taylor, Cora. (1992). *The Doll.* Vancouver, BC: Douglas & McIntyre.

A Final Note about Magazines

There are many fine children's magazines available that captivate readers of all ages. This type of reading material is generally colorful, full of inviting games, activities, and illustrations, and lots of fun for kids. Some of our favorites include the following. (A more complete list can be found in Donald Stoll's book, *Magazines for Kids and Teens.*)

Reading magazines

MAGAZINES FOR AGES BIRTH TO SIX YEARS

Baby Bug   *Crayola Kids*
Humpty Dumpty   *Les Belles Histoires*
Sesame Street Magazine

MAGAZINES FOR AGES SIX TO ELEVEN YEARS

Boys' Life   *Chickadee*   *Creative Kids*
Girl's Life   *Highlights for Children*   *Jack and Jill*

Kids for Saving Earth News   Ranger Rick
Stone Soup: The Magazine by Young Writers and Artists
Troll Magazine   Wild   Zoo Books

MAGAZINES FOR AGES EIGHT TO FOURTEEN YEARS
Bonjour   Children's Digest   Cricket Magazine
Earth Savers   Hopscotch: The Magazine for Girls
New Moon: The Magazine for Girls and their Dreams
Odyssey   Owl Magazine   Ranger Rick
Soccer JR   Sports Illustrated for Kids
Superman and Batman magazines

MAGAZINES FOR AGES FOURTEEN AND UP
Allons-y!   Black Belt For Kids   Career World
Coins Magazine   Current Science   I Love English
In Motion   Karate/Kung Fu Illustrated
National Geographic   READ Magazine   Teen Beat
Teen Life   Visions   Western Horseman
YES Magazine   YM (Young and Modern)

Hints on What to Read with Your Children

 Birth to Two Years. Choose sturdy, colorful books in plastic, cardboard, and cloth.

 Ages Three to Six. Choose picture books (with no words), books with elaborate story lines, alphabet and number books, poetry, and information books.

 Ages Seven to Ten. Choose simple chapter books, but continue with picture books.

 Ages Eleven and Up. Even if you no longer read books with your children, read the same books they read and discuss the events and characters together.

 All Ages. There is a wide variety of magazines for all ages to enjoy together and independently.

Chapter Six: What You May Be Concerned About (Questions and Answers)

Q: I don't have time to read with Jason. I have three other kids at home and every one of them is busy. Even Jason has Tae Kwon Do three nights a week. I'm lucky to get everyone to sit down to dinner together some nights. Isn't it the teacher's job to teach my child to read?

A: We all have busy lives but it is important to pause on occasion and reevaluate our priorities. Extracurricular activities are important in the total development of our children, but it is a fact that reading to and with our children is the single most important factor in future reading/writing success. Reading and writing ability in turn predicts school success. Perhaps you might try getting family members together for "Reading Time" once a week. If someone misses part of the story, then the others can tell him or her about it before the next get-together. This kind of activity helps to build comprehension and listening skills. As well, you might want to investigate the availability of talking books at your local library. They can help to make the endless trips to and fro valuable listening time.

Q: I have been watching Devlin, a neighbor boy, read. He tries to sound out every word. That makes sense. I was taught to read like that, but my son Aaron doesn't seem to use this method. Oh, he can do it if I remind him but he seems to just recognize words. Others he just guesses at. Who is right? Which child will be a better reader?

A: Devlin is using phonics as his primary reading strategy. This is the way most of us were taught to read. Aaron, however, sounds as if he is using a combination of strategies. Our guess is that when asked to explain his method of reading he would say "I just recognize the words." This recognition is based on a number of methods including:

- recognizing words on sight;
- using clues like the length or shape of a word, the beginning letters, or the meaning of the passage to predict what the word might be.

In addition, competent readers, like Aaron, tend to skip over unknown words until the meaning from the rest of the sentence helps them to identify the unfamiliar word. Neither child is right or wrong. Who will be the better reader? At this point it is impossible to tell. Both will need encouragement and support in their chosen strategies and both need to realize that there are other strategies.

Q My daughter and I were reading a book last night called, *Momma Do You Love Me?* She was doing really well until she got to the word "mukluk." She tried to sound it out and couldn't make any sense of it. Then she looked at the picture. "Oh I know!" she said "moccasins" and carried on. They aren't even close. Should I have made her go back and really read that word?

A Your daughter is demonstrating the art of meaningful substitution. At some point in her background and experience she has seen or heard the word moccasin. She knows that these are a type of shoe or boot crafted by native people. In this story, set in the Arctic, the main characters are aboriginal. Thus it would make sense that their boots are also called moccasins. Her substitution did not change the meaning of the story. Thus it did not make sense to stop the flow of the tale for this correction. Once the story is over you might want to return to this page and explain the subtle difference between the two. This might, in fact, lead to an interesting discussion.

Q My son is nearing the end of grade one. He seems to like reading and wants to read out loud a lot. The problem is mine. It drives me crazy to listen to him read in that slow choppy monotone. Is this a stage he is in or do I invest in earmuffs?

A In our experience all but a few children go through this stage at some time in their early reading development. It is due to the enormous investment of energy the child pours into using their newly learned skills. As a result he is unable to think about the finer points of expressive reading at the same time. With confidence and practice this stage soon passes. Try your best to maintain your enthusiasm. Treasure even these moments because they will pass quickly.

Q Is it wrong for kids to make up stories from pictures? Sara who is in the first few months of grade one can't really read her books but she thinks she can.

A Reading activity begins long before children recognize their first word. Important prereading activities include watching parents and others read and write, listening to stories, connecting the illustrations with the text, showing an interest in the text, and pretending to read a book themselves as they turn the pages and "say" the story. Classroom reading instruction builds these skills. It sounds as though Sara is on her way to becoming a competent reader. Over the next months you will observe her growing ability to recognize many words, make connections between sounds and letters, and realize that the words on the page go together to make meaning. In short she will become a reader.

Q Have you ever run into a child that has read the same book so many times that he has it memorized? My six-year-old son Nathan says he is reading and he is repeating the text word for word, but he is staring at the refrigerator door, for heaven's sake. If I get after him he gets in a huff. This doesn't seem like reading to me. What can I do?

A Frequently, young children have favorite books they come back to over and over. They become familiar with the book and appear to enter right into the story. The words, patterns, and pictures become almost second nature to them. This involvement is integral to developing Nathan's confidence. As he gets older he may want to read only books on one topic, dinosaurs for example, or all of the books in a series, or perhaps only books by one author. All of this is a natural part of children's growth as readers. It is important to allow Nathan to assert himself at this point. As you have learned, pushing him in another direction only results in friction. When the child is ready to move on, then you can make suggestions. In reading development, it is usually wise to take your cues from the child.

My baby is nine months old. Is it too early to read to her?

 We have said it before but it bears repeating. The single most important thing parents can do is read to their children, regardless of their age. Start today. It doesn't have to be a children's book. Lay your baby on the bed and read aloud to her from an adult selection. Babies learn a great deal from hearing the patterns of language in the words of a trusted adult. You, in turn, gain a little valuable self time. A good friend used to read aloud to her children as they were nursed. Her oldest child was weaned on Margaret Atwood, her second on Alice Walker. Neither appears to have suffered any ill effects.

 Do I have to buy a lot of books so that my baby will become a good reader? We can't really afford many.

This question is more a reflection of our consumer society than of children's needs. Public libraries are full of excellent books that can be accessed for only a few dollars. Garage sales and flea markets provide another good supply. Remember that books are only one part of the equation in early reading development. The second vital component is the involvement of a trusted adult. Invest your time rather than your money and you will reap tremendous rewards.

Mackenzie, my niece, is seven months younger than my Sam and she can read. He doesn't even know if a book is right-side up yet. What have we done wrong?

Children learn at individual and varying rates. Some children, like Mackenzie, show remarkable growth over a short period of time, while others, like your son, take longer to reach the same level of language development. Regardless of what level they are working at, or how quickly they learn, children need to experience success, meet with challenges that move them on to learning something new, and be recognized for their efforts and progress. In reading, as in all things, children's self-esteem and their ability to learn is enhanced by their own feeling of accomplishment and by others having a positive regard for their achievements. In short, you have not done anything wrong. Love him and support him and he will be just fine. At some point he may outshine Mackenzie in some other area.

Q: Here is my daughter's report card. It says "Jenna reads well but has trouble with comprehension." What does that mean? How can I help her?

A: By definition, reading includes understanding. Children must be able to do more than just say the words they see in print. They need to comprehend what they have read and what it means. There are a variety of reasons why children do not understand what they read. Some children believe that reading is simply learning to say the words on the page. Children can become skilled at figuring out words, paying little attention to what they mean. When children have to struggle too much with the words, they understand little of what they've read. The material may have content or vocabulary the children have difficulty relating to. Children need background knowledge on which to build understanding. Ask your daughter's teacher to assess whether any of these reasons may be appropriate. It is likely that your child is reading material that is too difficult for her. By developing a good relationship with your child's teacher, you take an important step towards helping your child to succeed in school.

Q: There are three grade one teachers at our school. Mrs. Brown says she teaches phonics. Mr. Bartlett teaches something called whole language. I heard that Mrs. Lawson just lets the kids read and write. How can I tell which will be the best classroom for my child?

A: It is likely that Mrs. Brown uses a variety of strategies in her classroom. However, she may believe that a strong grounding in phonics, that is, the matching of letters to sounds, is necessary to successful early reading development. Whole Language teachers like Mr. Bartlett believe that children should learn to read and write in ways that begin with stories and then work back towards identifying words, letters, and sounds. For this teacher, language is seen as a way of communicating meaning and ideas, rather than as a collection of separate components (letter, sounds, symbols, etc.). As children experience success, a foundation is built. New concepts are added to this foundation. Language is always used for a purpose and children begin reading books and writing on their own as soon as they are interested. Now consider Mrs. Lawson's classroom. Many teachers are now incorporating their whole language philosophy and strategies into an organizational structure called Readers' and Writers' Workshops. These activities differ in each classroom and are simply vehicles for implementing whole language ideas.

You are your child's first and most important teacher. You know her better than anyone else. Keep this information in mind and visit each of the classrooms. Talk to the teachers. Ask questions such as, "How much do children read while in school? How do you teach phonics? Does my child understand what she reads? How does my child's reading ability compare to that of other children her age?" Whatever your choice for the next year continue to maintain a high level of involvement. Parents and teachers working together are the power team in education.

Why can my grandson David read big words like *elephant* and *computer* but still have trouble with little words like *the, there, went,* and *where*?

Children most easily remember words that are of special importance to them, regardless of their length or complexity. David may be interested in elephants. Perhaps his class has been reading a story about an elephant or is studying Africa. He may have heard Mom and Dad talking about the purchase of new computer or computer time may be a bonus for working hard in his classroom. Words like **the, there, went,** and **where** don't have much meaning in themselves. It is through continued experience with reading and writing that these become recognized as the words that connect ideas. Gradually, children learn to recognize them by sight. A word of caution. Spelling often develops in a similar fashion. With time and experience, spelling ability will develop.

Helping Your Child Learn to Read, Write, and Speak

How can I know if my child is reading at the level she should be?

 We have found that when parents talk about the "right level" they are referring to their child's progress in relation to other children in the same year of school. This information is often included in report cards. Talk to your child's teacher to gain a further understanding of your child's comparative performance. While this information is valuable, it is important to keep in mind that all children learn at individual and varying rates. In any classroom there will be children performing at a wide variety of different levels. Teachers recognize differences in children's language development and plan accordingly.

writing—

all children

do it

"Children want to write. They want to write on the first day they go to school. This is no accident. Before they get to school they mark up walls, pavements, and newspapers with crayons, chalk, pens, or pencils ... anything that makes a mark. The child's marks say 'I am.'"(p. 3, Graves, 1988)

Section Two: Writing—All Children Do It

This section offers parents a variety of activities designed to get children to write and keep writing. Real examples of young children's writing are provided to show that scribbling and drawing are all early attempts at writing. As computers enter the picture at home and at school, there are a variety of activities and programs that can be adapted to various age and developmental levels.

Naturally, many parents are concerned about two areas that have come to be associated with writing: spelling and phonics. Here, we outline what teachers are trying to accomplish with their instruction in these two areas and why different teachers stress different concepts. As before, a comprehensive question and answer section follows, highlighting such queries as, "What do I say to my child when I can't read his/her writing?" or "My child is five years old and can't write his/her name yet. Should I be worried?"

Chapter Seven: How Children Learn About Writing

Children are viewed as writers almost from the first moment they pick up a crayon and scribble across a surface.

Most adults were taught reading in grade one classrooms long before writing was even attempted. Presently, however, our children are viewed as writers almost from the first moment they pick up a crayon and scribble across a surface. Unfortunately, some children find walls to be the most attractive places to begin their writing careers. As a result, there are even washable crayons to use. Regardless of the surface they first choose—wall or paper—or the writing implement—crayon or lipstick—they are still beginning to learn about writing.

Scribbles Have Meaning

Parents are eager to see what very young children will "create" when given paper and crayons. These creations tend to be viewed as scribbles, a meaningless but pleasurable activity. Yet, as early as eighteen months, children may produce varying scribbles for writing and for drawing.

As is shown in this sample of a two-year-old's drawing, the scribbles are usually large and round.

Creating on paper

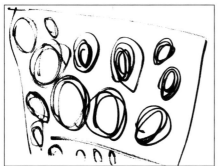
Scribbles have meaning (two-year-old)

The drawing and writing scribbles in this four-year-old's picture, below, tend to look more like conventional writing—lines, squiggles, and dots on a page. If a child sees lots of print in his early

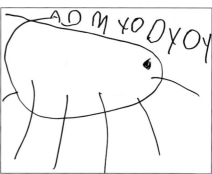

years and has a caregiver who points out letters and words, by age four or five his writing begins to take on letter-like shapes.

Drawing and Writing Tools

Writing taking shape (four-year-old)

One of the most important things parents can do is have materials readily available.

When trying to expose children to drawing and writing, one of the most important things parents can do is have materials readily available. These may include paper, newsprint, chalkboards, crayons, pencils, and markers. It is handy to store these items in a box or a low-standing kitchen drawer so that a child can choose to draw or write anytime without having to ask permission to get paper and other supplies. By providing your child with her own table or desk, she is more likely to begin drawing or writing at her leisure.

Writing materials can be expensive, however, there are ways to cut costs. For instance, print shops or newspaper offices often give away or sell roll-ends of newsprint or recycled paper at a fraction of its cost. Also, watch for recycled paper available from most businesses. As for other materials, back-to-school sales mean good values on crayons, markers, and paint. Grandparents and other family members could be asked to purchase these kinds of items for birthdays or other special occasions. But remember, parents need not spend a lot on these materials. Really all that matters is that children can find and use a variety of writing materials whenever they want to.

Children want to try a variety of writing tools. Small hands need to manipulate both fat and skinny tools. They feel the need to experiment with whatever they can find, much to parents' dismay. Very young children can be helped to draw with finger paint, shaving cream (with a little food coloring added for interest), or with sand poured into a shallow box. A friend's daughter, thinking she had found some new crayons, used the contents of a make-up bag to "write" on the bathroom mirror. She explained that she was writing "hello" to mom and dad, knowing this was the first place they looked on waking up in the morning. One way to deal with this is to hide all your make-up or other "writing" tools that you deem inappropriate. Another way is to provide a variety of attractive writing tools for your child. Eventually and thankfully, they will succumb to parents and teachers who encourage them to use pencils and crayons.

What You Do Affects Your Child's Writing

Sometimes when children bring their drawings to us it is hard to know exactly what to say. We don't want to say something like, "What a nice picture of a dog!" since that may not be what the child had in mind at all. Try saying, "What a lovely drawing! Tell me all about it." This allows the child to describe his creation and allows you to make other related comments like, "What kind of dog is it? What's the dog doing? I really like dogs, too!"

If possible, display your child's art or writing. Even putting it on the refrigerator with a magnet shows your child that you are proud of his efforts. Another way to display your child's work is to hang it on a bulletin board either in the child's bedroom or in another central location. On a recent Oprah Winfrey episode, an interior decorator suggested framing special pieces to display in your home.

Children learn about writing by watching you.

Children learn about writing by watching you. Most of us write at some point during our day. We write checks, make grocery lists, compose lists of things to do, write birthday cards and letters to friends or relatives, or leave notes for spouses and older children. Whenever you are doing one of these activities, let your child in on the activity by telling him what you are doing. For example, "I am writing a check to pay for our lights and water. I sign my name at the bottom to show the people who is paying the bill/money."

Robin's daughter, Amy, noticed that her mom's and dad's signatures differed greatly—one was easy to read and the other was a fancy scribble. As a result, she decided to practice her own signature until she had perfected one she really liked. Through these kinds of activities, a child learns that writing is an essential part of a person's life.

Reading and writing development go hand in hand. A child who has been read to a lot will likely develop as a writer with considerable ease. This is why, when children are learning to write stories, they will often try out the writing styles of various authors in their own writing. It is not uncommon for primary-aged children to use a line like "This kid is driving me crazy!" (from Robert Munsch, popular children's author) in their own stories.

Notes and Signs

> **Children love to receive notes. A personalized message makes them feel special and shows them that you have confidence in their abilities to figure out what you have written.**

Children love to receive notes. A personalized message makes them feel special and shows them that you have confidence in their abilities to figure out what you have written. They will try to read notes written to them even if they are not yet reading. This activity need not be time-consuming. For example, you can use scraps of paper to leave a note by the bathroom sink under his toothbrush, "Tim, please brush your teeth! Love, Mom" or a note on your child's pillow that says, "Travis, you did a great job cleaning up your bedroom. Love, Dad." Even children who can't read will bring the note to you and ask, "What does this say?" A very young child might need you to say, "Did you get the note I left for you?" and "Let's go find it and read it together." Reading the note together encourages even more reading and writing as they may wish to respond by writing a reply.

Children often write notes because they hope parents or siblings will write back to them. If your child shows an interest in writing to you, then try starting a home journal. Your child can write you a message at bedtime and you can read it and write back. She will likely eagerly anticipate reading your note at breakfast. For older children who may come home from school to an empty house, a note is a way to welcome them.

Another of the many writing activities children like to do is writing notes or signs to put on a bedroom door. A friend's four-year-old daughter made this sign that reads: "Nobody allowed in my room."

Parents will first notice the errors in spelling on this sign.

The message is clear even if the spelling is not.

However, it would not be helpful to point out these errors when first reading the sign. This child's message is clear even with spelling errors. Your child needs you to say something about *what* the message says before you comment on *how* it is written.

Be Patient

Children first must learn that writing has a purpose; that is, it tells or communicates a message to another person. Later, school-aged children become aware that correctness and neatness are important in conveying their messages. At this point, parents need to remember that learning anything new takes time and they themselves made mistakes while learning. Learning to drive a car, play a new sport, understand a new job—all take time and effort. We expect to make mistakes along the way and we realize these occur until we master the new skill.

Learning to write takes time and practice.

The same principle of learning applies to learning how to write. Mistakes are important to learning. If a child only writes down on paper those words and letters that are perfect, then she would not write much at all. Therefore, parents need to accept what their children have written first. Statements like, "Read me your message" or "That's an interesting story" are good places to begin. These statements show the importance of talk in learning to write and draw.

Chapter Eight: How Children Learn to Write

Resist the temptation to move your child quickly from one stage to another.

In the beginning, very young children are playing when they write or draw on a page. We like to think of play as the work of children. Their lines and scribbles may not mean much to parents but children can tell us a lot about what they create.

Many researchers agree that children learn to write in fairly consistent ways. The following stages and samples of a child's writing show one way that writing develops. You may wish to compare these samples to your child's writing to see which stage his writing resembles. Resist the temptation to move your child quickly from one stage to another. Remember, as a colleague of ours once said, "It takes six years to make a six-year-old!" Pressuring your child to progress too quickly may actually be detrimental to his development. These stages are generally followed by children as they experiment with writing.

Writing begins with playing on paper.

Stages of Writing Development

- 📖 Playing on paper
- 📖 Trying symbols
- 📖 Discovering letters
- 📖 Aha! **Mommy** starts with **m**
- 📖 Moving toward "the right way"

Playing on Paper

In the beginning, children play on paper with crayons, pens, or markers. Not long after discovering that the marks on the page are their own, children begin chatting while they write. They might be telling what is happening in their picture or talking to someone they have drawn. At this stage, children's drawing means something to them while they are actually creating it. A day or two later, they may not be able to recall what it is.

Playing on paper

This sample was produced by a three-year-old whose Dad overheard his son talking about a moose while drawing. This shows the importance of talk in learning to write and draw.

Trying Symbols

As children continue to be exposed to the written word, they begin to make letter-like marks on their pages among the drawings and scribblings, including lines, dots, circles, and squiggles. These are their first attempts at writing their own names or words they have seen around them (environmental print). As you can imagine, **M** for **McDonald's** is a popular choice. Remember that during this stage, when children are between three and five years of age, they are experimenting. It is quite likely that they will print letters sideways, upside-down, and backwards. Such experimentation is normal and natural. It should not be viewed as a problem. It may be helpful to compare the way children view letters to the way they see a spoon on the counter. They know it is a spoon whether it is upside-down, sideways, or otherwise positioned. At first, letters are seen in a similar way by children. Later, when a child is eight or nine years old, and if she is still reversing letters on a regular basis, then the teacher may suggest some strategies to try at home.

Below, the two writing samples of a six-year-old show how natural it is for children to experiment with letters. In the example on the left letters accompany lines and in the example on the right they accompany a picture. These samples show that the child recognizes that words can go together with lines as they may appear on a page of writing or with pictures as they may appear in a storybook. In each case the child's writing reflects her experiences with the world of print.

Trying symbols and lines   Putting together letters and pictures

Discovering Letters

To really understand what children are thinking about writing, it is necessary to talk with them about what they are doing.

Once children have been experimenting with letters for some time, they will use them more regularly in their "writing" and "drawing," sometimes filling the page and other times accompanying a picture. You may notice some consistencies about the writing of a young child who is just discovering letters. First, children often use letters from their own names or from those of brothers, sisters, mom, or dad. They typically learn the first letter of a name and write this for the entire word—**m** for **mom**. These letters are meaningful to them. Secondly, many children write capital letters in the beginning. This is because most of the print they see on signs, billboards, and in stores (environmental print) is written in capital letters.

Some children will begin making up their own words, for example, **G a r L** means **house**. At this stage, it is not important to try to teach your youngster that the word **house** begins with the letter **h**. It is more important to understand that your child is trying to convey a message in print. Simply ask your child to tell you about his writing or drawing and praise his efforts.

To really understand what children are thinking about writing, it is necessary to talk with them about what they are doing. A pair of researchers discovered how one five-year-old thinks about writing when she said, "Write my name. But you have to make it longer because yesterday was my birthday."

In this sample of a four-year-old's writing, row upon row of letters are produced. A child feels a wonderful sense of accomplishment with this type of activity because he can show others his writing skills or because he is able to communicate his thoughts by writing them for others to read.

Discovering letters

"Aha! Mommy and Mcdonald's Start with M!"

Some children who become aware too early that they are not writing "correctly" will stop writing letters altogether.

It is exciting when children begin to recognize that sounds and letters go together. At this stage they can relate some letters to sounds but they are not able to recognize or hear all the letters or sounds in a word. As might be expected, beginning consonants are easiest to recognize. These may be used to represent an entire word. Later, final consonants are added and later still, middle consonants. Examples of this include, writing **u** for **you**, **c** for **see**, **lik** for **like**, **sp** for **stop**. Vowels are usually the last to appear. This kind of matching takes a great deal of effort on the child's part and it is important to give him positive comments along the way. Many children, if not given assurances and support at this stage, become frustrated and turned off writing, especially if they think they cannot do it right. They cannot be spontaneous in their writing or drawing if they learn to constantly check with you to see if they have it right. As a result, they lose confidence in their own abilities to write or draw. Some children who become aware too early that they are not writing correctly will stop writing letters altogether.

Reinventing language

Notice in this five-year-old's drawing and writing that she has spelled some words correctly—**Amy**, **Mommy**, **Daddy**, **Lucy**. She told her mom she was writing "Amy goes (meaning 'says') Happy Birthday. Mommy goes Happy Birthday, Daddy goes Happy Birthday, Lucy goes Happy Birthday." Her writing includes inventive spelling for **goes**, and for **Happy Birthday** yet the message is still clear and her efforts are to be commended.

Some teachers call this stage the "reinvention of language" because it looks as if children are inventing the spellings of words as they write. You may hear your child's teacher talk about "inventive spelling" as part of a child's natural development toward becoming a writer. It may be your wish to see your children learn to write letters and words correctly the first time; however, research shows that it is more important to allow children to develop this knowledge on their own, with some help from supportive parents. For example, if a child is struggling to write the letters for **sh** and asks for the letter that makes this sound, then say, "The **s** and **h** together make **sh**." Or if a child asks "How do you write **bed**?", then try offering, "Say the word slowly and write down what you hear." It is likely that a six-year-old will write **bd** or **BD**. Then say, "Great, you heard two important sounds in that word," and leave him to continue his writing. Try to achieve balance between allowing children to sound out words for themselves and helping them when they ask for it.

writing—all children do it

This four-year-old has drawn a picture of her family celebrating a birthday. Notice how she labels the people in the picture. This combination of writing and drawing seems to be natural for many children.

Moving Toward "The Right Way"

As children write with confidence, many of their words become what teachers call "the standard version." For

Mommy and **McDonald's** start with **M**

example, over time, **luv** becomes **love**. However, this is a long stage. It is not uncommon for some children to be using inventive spelling for some words well into fifth or sixth grade. A child's progress away from inventive spelling depends upon how she has been supported in the previous stages. It is a healthy sign if your child uses both standard spellings and inventive spellings in her writing. If she only uses those words that she knows how to spell correctly, then she will use only a limited number of words and thus be unable to express her thoughts completely to communicate all she wishes to say. But if she tries many interesting and new words, even if she does not know how to spell them, then she is developing as a creative writer.

On the following page is an example of a story written by Robin's six-year-old daughter. Both the original version and the standard version are included.

Amy is experiencing the last two stages just described. She uses many standard spellings such as **day**, **dad**, **to**, and **the**. She tries less familiar words by writing beginning consonants and sometimes final consonants. She uses **h** for whole, **tm** for **time**, and **hr** for **her**. She attempts even more difficult words through more invention. It is exciting to see her spelling of **libare** because she has included all the major consonant and vowel sounds. The spelling of **then** is also interesting because Amy tries two different ways of spelling this word. First, **zen** and **dt**. On her third try, she begins with a **t** and this seems to be the clue she needs to sound it out or recall the word from memory. Through trial and error, she eventually discovers the standard spelling of **then** for herself. Parents who help their children in the ways described in this chapter will find that their young children become involved in writing tasks and develop personal self-help strategies while writing.

Amy's original

The Book is Lost

From: Mom's Daughter

To: Alyssa

One day Amy's Dad took her to the library.

And Amy got lost so Amy decided to look around.

Then she read a book that she liked and the book got lost. "Oh, no," said Amy.

Then Amy's Dad came. "Dad, dad, dad, dad, dad, dad, please, please, find the book for me." "Okay," said Amy's Dad.

The book was only behind the cupboard the whole time.

Then Amy and her Dad went home.

The standard version

From Your Child's Teacher

Remember that writing often comes from speech. When adults write letters, they will say a line over in their heads and then write it down. Children do the same thing. But the words they can say and understand are more sophisticated than the words they can write correctly. Consequently, one would expect to see a mix of both standard and inventive spellings in a piece of writing. At ages nine through eleven we would finally expect to see mostly standard spelling in our children's writing and that would likely come after a piece of writing has been revised and edited by the child in conference with a teacher or a peer.

Achieving standard spelling

Here is a five-year-old's Christmas wish list. Notice the mix of standard and inventive spelling. Her list includes: *Puppy Surprise, Creepy Crawlers, Monster Face, Barbie Lambourgini, Mama Having a Baby, Sally Secrets,* and *Aladdin Game.* It is likely that the correctly-spelled words are those this young writer is most familiar with. This familiarity comes from the home, the environment, and of course, advertising.

Standard and inventive spellings

Helping Children Develop As Writers

- Provide lots of different writing tools for your child to try out.

- Display your child's art and writing around the house.

- Leave notes for your child to read.

- Comment on *what* your child has written before saying anything about *how* it is written.

- Point out words and letters in the environment—Stop and Yield signs, names of department and grocery stores, and places of interest in the neighborhood.

- Ask your child to tell you about his drawing or writing so you can see the thinking and ideas that contributed to his creation.

- Balance allowing children to sound out words for themselves and helping them when they ask for it.

Chapter Nine: What the Teacher Does and Why

As children progress through the elementary and junior high grades, they do more and more independent writing. Students in schools mostly write using a series of steps educators call **The Writing Process**. These steps are not used for every piece of writing a child produces. Rather, they are used as a guide to help children see how writers get started and how they eventually publish a piece of writing. The diagram below shows one version of **The Writing Process**. Note that many of the arrows are double-sided, meaning that many aspects of the process are not sequential steps, but rather are intertwined.

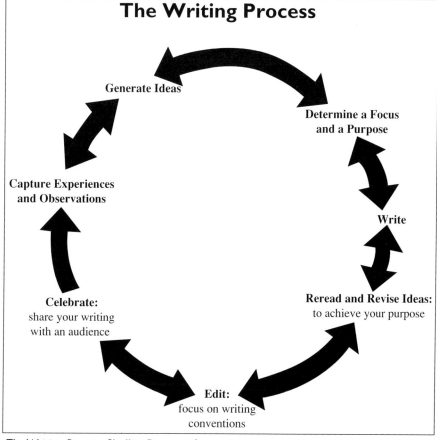

The Writing Process, Shelley Peterson*

---

*Peterson, Shelley. (1995). *Becoming Better Writers*. Edmonton, AB: FP Hendriks Publishing Ltd.

The Writing Process

The main stages in the writing process are:

1. **Prewriting**. In the prewriting stage, children are encouraged to decide on a topic. They do this by brainstorming, making lists, looking at pictures, and talking about experiences.

2. **Drafting**. During the drafting stage, the child writes and writes and writes. Some children seem to need a quiet place to do this while others like to "talk out" their ideas with a friend as they go along. Many teachers believe that this is not the time to teach spelling or grammar. Rather it is the time to allow children to get all their ideas down on paper without worrying about "correctness." Often during this stage children make more spelling mistakes than usual because they are concentrating on telling their stories. This behavior does not mean your child's writing is returning to an earlier stage. It simply means that he is focusing on the creative part of writing for this time.

3. **Revising**. In school older children are encouraged to revise or rewrite parts of their stories to make them clearer or to communicate their ideas better. In many classrooms, children work in pairs or with the teacher to revise their writing. Published writers know it is often easier for someone else to see where they can make their ideas clearer. For example, a grade three student writes about her characters in one setting and then suddenly moves them to another place. In this case, a teacher or a peer might ask the student to describe how the characters got from one place to another. Through the act of telling a partner what happened, the student often realizes her lack of clarity or the teacher may say, "You need to write down what you just told me."

Student-teacher writing conference

From Your Child's Teacher

Revising is used sparingly or not at all with younger writers.

Revising is used sparingly or not at all with younger writers. Over-correction may cause young writers to become frustrated and unhappy with having to make too many changes to a story that was hard to write in the first place. The physical act of writing for a long period of time (even ten to fifteen minutes) can be hard work for six- and seven-year-olds.

4. **Editing**. This is where the student and the teacher correct spelling, punctuation, and grammar. As a first step for all writers, a teacher may suggest that students look for errors themselves and draw a line under the words or groups of words that do not look or sound right in the story. Very young children (six- to eight-year-olds) are often able to recognize spelling errors even if they are not able to tell you how they should be spelled.

Editing together

Older children can also begin to make their own corrections by sounding out words, rereading them, learning to use the dictionary, getting help from a friend or a teacher or using the spell-checker on the computer. It is important to remember that children have varying capabilities for handling corrections. The child who finds writing a chore and who struggles for days to complete a story because of problems with printing or finding ideas may be frustrated and angered by having to do a lot of editing. Perhaps this child will spend only fifteen minutes correcting his writing. Another child, however, who finds writing easy and completes a story in a day may be encouraged to spend more time revising and editing the story. Since less time and energy was spent on creating the story, more time can be spent on other stages in the writing process.

5. Publishing. Many teachers and their students enjoy seeing the final copies of their writing displayed or published. They realize that students are proud to have their work displayed for others to see. Doing so fulfills one of the purposes for writing—communicating ideas to an audience. Teachers sometimes post stories on bulletin boards, make booklets of students' stories, or have students read their stories aloud in class. You can do the same thing at home by sitting down next to your child while she reads her story to you. Remember that you are likely her most important audience and what you think matters to her a great deal!

Preparing a piece of writing for publishing

The Writing Process

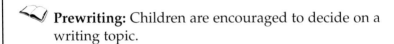 **Prewriting:** Children are encouraged to decide on a writing topic.

Drafting: Children write their pieces, focusing on their ideas.

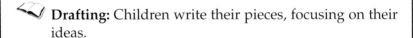 **Revising:** Children go back over their writing and rewrite parts to make their ideas clearer to a reader.

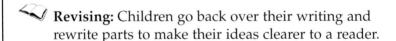 **Editing:** Children work on their writing to correct spelling, punctuation, and grammar.

Publishing: Children display their writing in some way so that it can be shared with others.

Chapter Ten: I Want My Child to Be a Good Speller

Spelling ability and writing ability go hand in hand. It is hard for a reader to enjoy a piece of writing that has many spelling mistakes. Knowing this, children who do not spell well can become frustrated with writing altogether. Each individual comes to an understanding about spelling in a different way. Some have always been good spellers and may not think about it much. Others have struggled with spelling as youngsters but have developed strategies to improve their spelling ability. Still others, who had difficulty with spelling as youngsters, continue to have difficulty. Since spelling is sometimes a hot topic, it might be useful to talk about how spelling is taught in classrooms and then think about ways to help children at home.

Teaching Spelling Using Weekly Tests

In some classrooms, spelling is taught much the same way it has been taught for many years. It is taught as a separate area in language arts. On Monday students receive a list of spelling words or they develop their own list to study throughout the week. The teacher may provide worksheets or activities to help students practice these words. On Friday students are tested on these words. This routine is well-established and many of us recognize it from our own schooling. For some children who are already good spellers and do not require a lot of instruction, the spelling test is a waste of time. They receive perfect weekly scores without much effort. However, even good spellers can and do spell their "spelling list" words incorrectly at other times—when writing a story or in a journal. One of the reasons this happens is because the child has learned to spell the word in isolation, that is, when it was not part of a sentence. Therefore, when the child writes the word in another place like in a sentence, he may not recognize the word and so does not apply what was learned from the spelling list. This is a common outcome of this type of teaching. It does not mean your child is lazy because she does not apply what has been learned through the spelling list. Actually, a child who consistently does well on weekly spelling tests is showing you that she is quite good at memorizing words that stand alone. Spelling words correctly that are surrounded by other words in a sentence or in a story in a completely different task.

Teaching Spelling with Writing

> **Teaching spelling is a balancing act. You want to encourage your child to look at her writing like a detective, to find the inventive spellings.... However, you do not want to destroy her pride in having created an interesting story or confidence in her ability.**

Many teachers are now teaching spelling as part of the many writing activities they plan for children. In these classrooms, children write a first draft and even a second draft (copy) of a story without worrying about correct spelling. It is believed that if children first think about their stories and their ideas, then their writing will be far more sophisticated and interesting. On the other hand, if students only write stories containing the words they know how to spell correctly, then their writing tends to be simplistic and does not show their true abilities.

After a first or second draft of their writing, the teacher then works individually with students to find and correct the spelling errors (sometimes called inventive spellings). Depending on the child and the number of nonstandard spellings, the teacher may not require that the student correct every error. To do so could overwhelm the student, who might then give up halfway through the piece or not even begin the corrections at all. Even worse is if the child is forced to correct every error only to hate his writing when it is done or come to hate writing in general. So teaching spelling is a balancing act. It is

Helping with spelling

important to encourage your child to look at her writing like a detective, to find the inventive spellings and to understand that correct spelling is important to clearly communicating her intended message. However, you do not want to destroy her pride in having created an interesting story or confidence in her ability.

Strategies for Helping Your Child with Spelling

Several good books have been published on teaching spelling if you wish to read more about this skill. These books are listed in Appendix 13. Here is a list of effective ways to help your child become a good speller.

1. **Read what your child has written.**

   a) When your child brings you something he has written, always read it all the way through first. Comment on the content or the purpose of the writing before pointing out any spelling errors.

   b) Begin by saying something specific related to what the story is about such as, "What an interesting story! I especially liked the part about…." or "Your story reminded me of the time…." When you begin this way, your child knows you are interested in *what* he has written.

   c) If the story appears to be in "rough" (draft) form, ask your child if he would like help with some spelling. Try saying, "It's a great story. If you'd like, I could help you with the spellings of some of the words." Always tell your child that he has done a good job sounding out a word, but say that some words are tricky. Show him an example from his story.

   d) The word may be "action" and your child has spelled it "akshun." You will want to tell your child that the letter **c** sometimes makes the same sound as **k**, and that this word has the letter **c** in it. Then say **shun** and write **tion**. Tell your child that the ending **tion** is how we write the sound **shun** even though it does not look like the sound it makes. If you say or sing the letters separately—**t-i-o-n**, your child may memorize this spelling right away. An older child may be able to correct the spelling of this word simply by having it pointed out. He may have been so involved in the ideas of the story that he was not concentrating on the spelling at first. Later, when he does not have to think so hard about getting ideas down, he will be able to spot obvious spelling errors.

2. **Use the "Three Tries" method.** When you and your child have found a word that is not spelled correctly, ask her to write out the word three different ways to see if she can find

the correct spelling. This strategy works well for students in grade four or beyond. Many students discover correct spellings this way because they are encouraged to try different spellings. Parents can help their children by showing them which one is correct or by showing them how to use the dictionary to find one of the spellings of the word.

3. **Picture the word in your head.** When a child is struggling with the spelling of a word, write the word correctly. Then, ask him to close his eyes and try to picture the word in his head. Then, have him write down what he sees. Doing this several times and checking the correctly spelled word each time may help him remember the word later.

4. **Draw a picture.** For children in grades one to three, it may be helpful to turn a word into a picture. For example, the word **look** could be drawn with two eyes. This reminds the child that the word is spelled with **oo** in the middle.

5. **Use Blocking.** As your child looks at a word, have her draw a box around it as shown, using the shape of the letters to guide her. For some children, the shape or box around the word is recalled the next time she uses it, thus aiding spelling.

    stop = stop
    look = look

    Blocking

6. **See it, say it, spell it.** This method asks the child to look at the word (see it), pronounce it aloud (say it), and repeat aloud the letters he sees (spell it). This can be done orally or written.

7. **Write the word in a sentence.** Have your child write the word in a sentence. For some children, seeing the word in a meaningful context, like a sentence, helps them to recall its correct spelling.

Spelling is an important skill and one that makes children's writing better. It enhances their ability to communicate ideas clearly. However, children do not become better spellers by memorizing words. They become better spellers by writing more, by trying to figure out some words independently, by asking others for help, by looking in books like dictionaries, and above all, by reading and being read to. It is natural to want to help your child become a better speller, but remember to accentuate the positive by commenting first on *what* your child has written rather than on the mistakes. Be selective about pointing out errors so that your child is not overwhelmed by the work needed to make his story perfect.

> **It can be a difficult experience when you see your child's writing come home from school with spelling errors. However, making mistakes is a natural part of learning something new.**

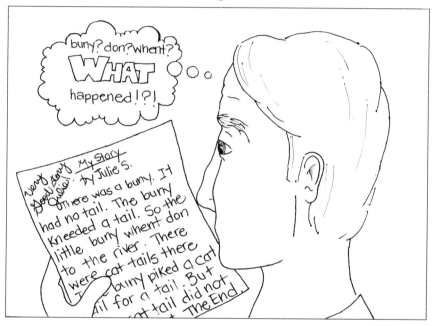

It can be a difficult experience when you see your child's writing come home from school with spelling errors. However, making mistakes is a natural part of learning something new. Learning to play a musical instrument, taking up a new sport, or putting together a new stereo are all exciting endeavors. But because these endeavors involve learning, learners are bound to make some mistakes along the way. Now that you have some understanding about how children are likely to be taught spelling in school, you may understand why not every error is corrected on a piece of writing. (Additional resources about teaching spelling are listed in Appendix 13.)

Chapter Eleven: Encouraging Daily Writing

There are many daily activities that parents can do with their children to support and encourage writing development. Many of these are natural family activities that take little planning or forethought. Yet they can make a real difference to a child's development as a writer.

Calendar

If possible, use a planning calendar with large squares for writing messages. Help your child write in special days, appointments, and other important activities. This can be displayed on the refrigerator for all to see and for your child to read daily.

Playtime

Make sure that your child has time in her day for free play with writing and drawing materials. By providing space and writing materials, your child can create personal projects and possibly use her writing skills in her play. If you have boxes of varying sizes, your child might (with your help) build a car, a store, a doctor's office, or a restaurant. If paper is available for these activities, then children can write prescriptions, take orders at the restaurant, make a grocery list, or write receipts for gasoline sales.

Always keep paper and pencils nearby. When children are old enough to answer the telephone on their own, they can take down phone messages for you and the rest of the family. Try to place paper and crayons where your child already likes to play—in a playhouse, in the kitchen, next to a car-racing set. She will likely find uses for it. For instance, your child might write a message she takes over the play phone or she may record the numbers of the race cars to show which one goes first. Children cannot choose to write if paper and pencils are not readily available. The more places you supply writing materials, the more often your child will find a reason to write.

Signs, Signs, and More Signs!

Once children begin to see the power of print, they may get a little carried away making signs to post all around the house. Not long after Robin brought home a new baby daughter, she noticed that visitors were extremely thoughtful, knocking at the door rather than ringing the bell. When she mentioned this to her family, her seven-year-old smiled and said she had written a note and put it on the front door telling

Signs and messages

everyone there was a new baby at their house. Children can also be encouraged to make other informative signs. "Kitchen Floor is Wet," "Quiet Time for Reading," "Do Not Touch the Pie," or "Be Home at 4:00 PM."

Thank-You Notes

Many parents like their children to write thank-you notes to relatives and friends but they get frustrated when this becomes a difficult chore. Sometimes writing is viewed by children as too hard when they know a parent is going to have them correct or fix everything they have done. Instead, write the thank-you note together. If you help your child with this activity the first few times, then he will get the idea and be able to do it on his own when he has gained writing skills. While he is young, however, you can help him make a card by folding a piece of paper in half and decorating the front with finger paint, felt pens, potato prints, magazine pictures, or a photograph. Inside the card, each of you could write a short message. Yours might say, "Thanks for the lovely boots for Sam. He likes wearing them on our walks." Your child then writes his own message that may include a picture if this is what your child wants to do. Make sure you address the envelope together and, if possible, make a special trip to the mailbox so that your child views this activity as having a purpose. Together you have created a thoughtful keepsake for someone. It is even better if the recipient acknowledges having received the note because it tells the child that writing is a vehicle for communication.

Confidence is important to how your child develops as a writer. The parents' role in helping a child feel comfortable and confident in writing is important. Remember that when you are responding to your child's writing or drawing, say, "Tell me about what you have done (written, drawn)." It allows him to explain the lines and scribbles in a way that does not make him feel that his creation is unclear or inadequate.

Homework Books (Agendas)

Some schools and teachers have students keep a homework book or an agenda where they record assignments, test dates, spelling words, and important notices or reminders. Parents may be asked to sign these and write comments on them each day before the child takes them back to school. Establishing a routine of reading the homework book together can be a real benefit to students who need to see the value of writing to organize themselves and to communicate with parents and teachers regularly.

School Reports

Older children are asked to work at home on school-related reports or projects from time to time. It can be difficult to know how to help with this kind of activity. Some children simply need to know that you are interested in their work. Try to set aside about 30 minutes to sit together to work on the report. Depending on your child, you may need to provide help with one or more of the following:

1. **Organizing information according to sub-topics.** For example, when writing a report on an animal, it is helpful to write information using sub-topics such as habitat, food, shelter, and young.
2. **Putting information into his own words.** Have your child read a passage. Close the book and have him tell you about what he just read.
3. **Using correct spelling, punctuation, and grammar.** Try not to make these skills the focus of your child's writing when he is working on a first draft. Wait until the writing is done. Then sit together and read through the report looking for errors in spelling, punctuation, and grammar. Let your child do most or all of the corrections himself.

When providing help with a report it is important to ensure that you are not doing the work for your child. Here are some suggestions on how to approach helping your child.

1. Listen to what your child wants to accomplish and what is required by the teacher for the assignment. If your child is not clear about the purpose or the requirements, you may then wish to talk to the teacher to clarify the purpose.
2. Remember that even though your child may not be able to explain his goals completely, he may still have an idea about what he wants to do. Try to help him clarify his goals by asking questions such as, What do you want to know about _____? Why do you want to know about that? How is it related to what you are studying in school?

Working on a school project

3. Watch for signs of frustration from your child. This may mean he has worked long enough on the project for one night, that he is frustrated at his lack of understanding (or yours), or because you are expecting more than he can handle at this time. Gage your child's ability to handle

information or ideas and try not to exceed what he can handle in one session.

4. Give your child time to work on his own. It will likely take him longer to do a task than it would take you, but remember that he is learning as much about *how* to do a report as he is learning about the topic of the report.

5. Work out a time line or work schedule together. Find out when the report is due and help your child decide what he can accomplish each night. This will help him organize his time so as not to be rushed at the last minute.

Both you and your child can benefit from working together on a project. If you start a routine of working together early, then helping in later years will be easier.

Encouraging Daily Writing

- **Calendar.** Display a large calendar on the refrigerator or on a bulletin board to write in special days, appointments, and other important activities.

- **Playtime.** Keep paper and writing materials out for your child to use when playing.

- **Signs.** Parents and children can leave notes for one another regarding phone calls, reminders, and other messages.

- **Thank-You Notes.** Together, parents and children can create thank-you notes for special people in their lives.

- **Homework Books (Agendas).** Keep track of you child's assignments, tests, spelling words, and important notes and reminders.

- **School Reports.** Provide help at home by setting aside time to supervise your child's work.

Chapter Twelve: What You May Be Concerned About (Questions and Answers)

Q: I can't read what my five-year-old Stacey writes. Just yesterday she brought me her latest story. It was a piece of paper folded in half with two pictures on it, some scribbles and groups of letters like *tttttt* and *oooo*. What do I say? How can I help her?

A: Stacey's story is entirely appropriate for a five-year-old child. It shows you that she understands that pictures and text together communicate meaning. Her scribbles and random groups of letters indicate a beginning awareness that shapes, called letters, are grouped in text. These shapes and their grouping are important to communicating meaning. The best strategy at this point is to begin with a specific compliment "I like this ... here," followed by the all-important comment "Tell me about your story."

You can help Stacey by providing her with a variety of materials to write with and on. Take advantage of opportunities to include written language in her day—lists, notes, phone numbers, messages. Be that all-important audience or correspondent that she needs to develop and refine her skills.

Q: Troy is just starting grade three. He brought home a story he had published. I was shocked that there were spelling mistakes! How come? Will he ever learn to spell properly?

A: There are good reasons why errors in children's work may be left uncorrected. The first relates to the developmental level of the child. Sometimes errors are left uncorrected because the writing, as it stands, represents the child's best work at his or her level of development. The writing is worthy of praise regardless of the errors.

The second reason for leaving errors uncorrected relates to the purpose or the activity and the intended learning. Children in classrooms are involved in many kinds of writing activities. It is important that you understand the purpose for the particular piece of writing. Teachers make different types of corrections depending on the purpose of the activity and what the student is to learn from it.

Teachers often keep portfolios of writing samples for each child. These samples are the best indicators of your child's growth. You may want to create your own memory portfolio at home. Lisa's 22-year-old son still delights in looking back over his early writing.

 My five-year-old is not holding the pencil properly. I have mentioned it to her teacher who does not seem concerned. He says that pencil grip often corrects itself. What do you think?

 Your daughter's teacher is right. As your daughter develops both gross motor and fine motor control it is likely that her pencil grip will evolve into one that more closely resembles the one you were taught. However, it is important to remember that, as in all levels of development, individual children mature at varying rates. If your child has completed the second grade and you are still uncomfortable with what you see, then there are a number of aids sold in teacher's stores designed to correct small problems.

 I am confused about neatness. When I went to school everything had to be just so. Now it seems that teachers accept anything. My kid's writing books are a real mess. I was taught to think carefully and then write. What has changed?

 In order to answer this question fairly we would have to know both the purpose this writing book is used for and the intended learning outcomes. For example, if the book in question is your child's journal or diary, these books tend to be personal and hence are not generally marked or corrected. At some points in the writing process it is appropriate to simply let ideas flow. These ideas may later be transformed into a draft for a particular piece of writing. Children can express themselves more freely initially and then later concern themselves with neatness, spelling, and grammar to make their writing easier for others to understand.

Q When do teachers begin to teach children handwriting? I am trying to teach Jennifer, who is in grade two, to write her name. She was proud as can be so she took it to school and showed her teacher. That day I got a note home asking me, in a nice way mind you, to please let the teacher handle at least the initial stages of handwriting instruction. What gives?

A In many schools children receive instruction in both printing and handwriting. Children first learn manuscript writing (printing.) Sometime between the ages of eight and ten, they are introduced to handwriting (cursive writing.) Both are developmental skills that children learn through direct instruction, following models and having purposeful situations in which they can practice and produce their best work. As a beginning teacher Lisa was asked for a sample of her own handwriting. From this sample it was pointed out that she was making several careless errors and was cautioned about passing them on to her students. Perhaps this is what your child's teacher is referring to. Asking the teacher directly would be the best strategy. At the very least the teacher should be able to provide you with a template to guide your work with your daughter.

Q Is spelling still taught in schools?

A Yes, children are still taught spelling in school. Children learn to spell in a variety of ways, which include a range of interesting reading and writing activities, weekly spelling lists developed by the teacher and based on words in use, individual spelling instruction built on words used in the children's personal writing, and spelling textbooks. In most classrooms a combination of these strategies will likely be in use. Children's attempts to represent words are commonly called temporary or invented spelling. They do not take the place of conventional spelling. However, children's experiments with spelling play a key role in their learning about written language. These invented spellings also provide valuable information for the teachers in planning lessons and activities that help children develop writing skills.

I notice a lot of simple spelling errors in my daughter's written work. Will I be interfering with the teacher's program if I try to teach some phonics at home?

One of the most powerful ways to teach spelling is with the words used in a child's personal writing. We can't imagine any teacher being concerned about a parent seizing this opportunity for a positive interaction with his or her child. Try to refrain, however, from being overzealous. In the early stages of writing development, children can become discouraged by too many corrections of their writing. They come to believe that they cannot "do it right," and often become afraid to try. A good rule of thumb at this stage is to limit corrections to a maximum of five.

We just bought a new computer. Will I be hurting my child's writing development if I let him use the computer to compose? Is there something sacred about pencil/pen and paper?

Many children in elementary schools today are also learning keyboarding skills. Some excellent software is now available for the home market so students have the opportunity to use computers for writing activities. Children are also often encouraged to use computers to add a professional touch to their written work. The use of typed presentations can be helpful for those children who experience difficulty with penmanship skills. However, there will always be times when penmanship is important so it should not be under-emphasized.

Grandma likes getting letters from my children, but I know the mistakes annoy her. Getting them to correct every mistake in their letters just takes the fun out of it. I'm really confused about how to handle this situation.

Try speaking directly to Grandma. Explain that the children's letters are treasured as representations of a child's best work at his or her level of development. Explain also that with her encouragement the children will become more competent in expressing their ideas in written form and learn more about spelling as they write more. In return, Grandma should try to respond as promptly as possible, also in written form. She might also be persuaded to include some pictures or some small item to brighten her grandchild's day.

Invented spelling can be difficult to read. You might ask your younger children to read the letter aloud to you before it is sent so that you can decipher the message.

Q My son likes to draw and he is good at it. What I'm worried about is that he seems to spend a lot of the time during Writer's Workshop illustrating his books. One time I visited the class and he was illustrating someone else's book as well. If writing is so important, wouldn't he be better off practicing what he doesn't do so well?

A One of the major premises of Writer's Workshop is that children are both authors and illustrators creating something important to share. We suspect that your son's teacher has spent some time discussing the role of illustration in successful picture books. It is not surprising that he chooses to display one of his talents in celebration of his text.

Another important aspect of Writer's Workshop is the collaborative nature of the writing process. In this context, it seems appropriate that your son would be asked to illustrate the text of another student. His contribution would be noted on the book jacket.

If you are still worried about the amount of time he seems to be spending on this activity, visit the classroom and discuss your concerns with the teacher. He may, in fact, need to be challenged to move on and learn something new.

Q My son gets *b*s and *d*s mixed up. Does this mean that he has a problem?

A Initially the direction the print goes or the order in which letters are placed does not seem important to young children. Their stuffed toy is recognizable whether they grab it by the head or leg or whether they put it in front of a chair or behind it. Many children naturally treat letters and words the same way with little concern about direction or order. Reversals (like your son's), mirror images (esuoh for house) or a different order of letters (sopt for stop) does not necessarily indicate a problem. Rather it is usually an early and temporary stage in learning to read and write. By the mid-elementary years, after much practice, most children leave these reversals behind.

For some children, reversals may persist into the upper elementary years. These children need direct teaching in combination with reading and writing activities to help overcome this problem.

What can I do to help my son with his writing?

A parent's main role is to encourage their children to write and to show an interest in what they have written. Talk to your child about the ideas he wants to express. Make sure your child sees you writing. Look for opportunities for your child to write in a variety of situations other than school assignments. Be positive. Applaud your child's effort and progress. Look for and respond to the ideas presented rather than the errors. Provide a suitable spot for writing and a variety of materials. Display your child's work prominently and collect samples to share at special time.

talking, listening, and learning

"[T]alking and learning go hand in hand. [Children] talk in order to achieve other ends: to share their interest in the world around them, to obtain the things they want, to get others to help them, to participate in the activities of the grown-up world, to learn how to do things or why things are as they are, or just to remain in contact." (Wells, 1986, pp. 53, 67)

Section Three: Talking, Listening, and Learning

The ability to express oneself orally and listen effectively is sometimes referred to as the overlooked skill in education. Yet listening and speaking competencies are essential for day-to-day living. Section Three describes how children learn to talk and how their efforts are supported or made problematic by those around them. A chart showing specific patterns of growth is provided along with many strategies, activities, and props to support literacy growth.

Chapter Thirteen: From Baby Babble to (Almost) Intelligible Conversation

Communication between you and your child is essential to your child's overall development.

Communication between you and your child is essential to your child's overall development. From young babies to conversant ten-year-olds, children are constantly refining their spoken language. But spoken language, like air, is all around us and we often take it and our ability to speak for granted. What, then, can parents do to support children as effective speakers and listeners?

Babies Communicate

It is never too early to begin talking to your baby as if she understands everything you say. Experts suggest that parents model normal speech instead of so-called baby talk. Parents are delighted when their babies first utter what sounds like "mama" or "dada." This seems to mark the beginning of a new phase—your child seems to be communicating with you verbally. A baby's cries are her first attempts at communication. She cries to tell you she is tired, hungry, lonely, or perhaps uncomfortable. Several months later, however, a baby learns to use certain sounds to communicate something specific. The unflattering term for this is baby babble. Although it does not sound like words at first, baby babble is the precursor to learning to talk. Many parents talk to their babies as if these young human beings are making perfect sense. In response to a child's babble, Dad says, "Did you say you'd like some milk? Okay, here's your cup." The child then takes the cup or throws it down. The parent responds accordingly. "Okay, no milk." Through trial and error the parent keeps talking to the child until he discovers what the child wishes to communicate. We all know how hard parents work at making sense of their babies' and toddlers' first utterances. One parent we know is convinced that when her baby points upstairs and calls, "Ah, ah, ah!" that she is calling for her sister, Ashley.

Talking to Babies and Toddlers

Here are a few tips for parents of babies and toddlers when it comes to developing speech.

1. If you have been told that you speak quickly, then try to slow down when speaking to your children. Some children combine words into phrases because of the way they hear them. "All of a sudden" becomes "allasudden," and of course, we know that many children think that *LMNO* is only *one* letter of the alphabet. They learn this because in speech, adults often speak quickly, which causes some confusion for children when they try to pronounce certain words. For most children, slowing down our own speech can help them later with understanding the spaces between words.

2. Talk out loud about what you are doing or what your child is doing. For example, if you put your baby or toddler in a high chair while you cook supper, keep talking while you work. "Now, daddy's going to make supper. First, we need some

carrots and a pot of water." And continue. Your child will not understand everything you say but he will eventually recognize many words and phrases related to the kitchen and cooking. Do the same at bath time, while changing the baby, when going for a walk, or during playtime. The more you talk to your baby, the quicker he will begin to talk back. (We know some of you are thinking, now *that's* a problem!)

3. Even very young babies can "take turns" when babbling. You speak, then wait for your child to speak before you speak again. Babies particularly like this and often make clicking noises with their tongues.

It is important to recognize that the incredible rate of learning that occurs between birth and age five is never again repeated in a child's life. Naturally the rate of development varies for each child, but your excited reaction at each stage will be evident to your child and will encourage their "work" in that stage.

The Development of Communication in Early Childhood*

The following table shows the stages of oral speaking development for children from birth to eight years.

Newborn
Cries; makes noncrying speechlike sounds, usually when feeding

1–2 months
Responds to human voice, which has a quieting effect; cries for assistance; makes pleasure sounds; distinguishes different (speech) sounds; makes more guttural or "throaty" cooing

3 months
Coos single syllable (consonant-vowel); turns head when hears a voice; responds vocally to speech of others; makes predominantly vowel sounds

4 months
Babbles strings of consonants; varies pitch; imitates tones; smiles at person speaking to him/her

5 months
Vocalizes to toys; discriminates angry and friendly voices; experiments with sounds; imitates some sounds; responds to name; smiles and vocalizes to image in mirror

6 months
Varies volume, pitch, and rate; vocalizes pleasure and displeasure such as squeals of excitement and intonations of displeasure

---

* From Stewig, J., & M. Jett-Simpson. (1995). Language Arts in the Early Childhood Classroom. Scarborough, ON: Wadsworth Publishing Co.

 From Your Child's Teacher

The Development of Communication in Early Childhood, continued

7 months
Plays vocally; produces several sounds in one breath; listens to vocalizations of others

8 months
Listens selectively; recognizes some words; repeats emphasized syllable; imitates gestures and tonal quality of adult speech

9 months
Produces distinct intonational patterns; imitates coughs, hisses, tongue clicks; uses social gestures

10 months
Imitates adult speech sounds if sounds are in child's repertoire; obeys some commands

11 months
Imitates inflections, rhythms, facial expressions

12 months
Recognizes own name; follows simple instructions especially if accompanied by a visual cue ("Bye bye"); reacts to "no" intonation; speaks one or more words; practices words she/he knows and inflection

15 months
Points to clothes, persons, toys, and animals named; uses words in conversation; has four- to six-word vocabulary

18 months
Begins to use two-word utterance; has approximately twenty-word vocabulary; identifies some body parts; refers to self by name; "sings" and hums spontaneously; plays question-answer with adult

21 months
Likes rhyming games; pulls person to show something; tries to "tell" experiences; understands some personal pronouns; uses I and mine

24 months
Has 200–300 word vocabulary; names most common everyday objects; uses short, incomplete sentences; uses prepositions (in, on) and pronouns (I, me, you) but not always correctly; uses some regular verb endings (-s, -ed, -ing) and plural -s but not always correctly; engages in short dialogues of a few turns about a topic

3 years
Has 900–1000 word vocabulary; creates three- to four-word sentences; uses "sentences" with subject and verb, but simple sentence construction; plays with words and sounds; follows two-step commands; talks about the present; shows rudimentary beginnings of turn taking in conversation by acknowledging partner with "yeah" and "uh-huh"

The Development of Communication in Early Childhood, continued

4 years
Has 1500–1600 word vocabulary; asks many questions; uses increasingly more complex sentence forms; recounts stories and the recent past; understands most questions about the immediate environment; has some difficulty answering how and why questions; relies on word order for interpretation

5 years
Has vocabulary of 2100–2200 words; discusses feelings; comprehends before and after regardless of word order; follows three-step commands; has ninety percent grammar acquisition; produces short passives; uses mostly direct requests and some indirect requests

6 years
Has speaking vocabulary of around 2600 words and a comprehension vocabulary of 20,000 to 24,000 words; comprehends parallel embedding in sentences and imperative commands; has many well-formed complex sentences; uses all parts of speech to some degree; identifies syllables; acquires rule for plural as in ropes, skis, and dishes; uses adverbial conjuncts now, then, so, and through; responds to indirect hints; keeps conversation going by elaborating on the topic

7 years
Comprehends because; follows adult ordering of adjectives; can use words left/right and front/back; is able to manipulate sound units to rhyme; recognizes unacceptable sound sequences; understands most relational terms; understands here, there, this, that, I, and you as referents in conversations

8 years
Uses full passives (eighty percent of children); is able to produce all English sounds; sustains concrete topics in conversation; begins considering others' intentions; little difficulty with comparative relationships; boasts, brags

Getting the Message Across

> **Some psychologists have told us that today's parents are spending less time talking with their children than in the past.**

Some psychologists have told us that today's parents are spending less time talking with their children than in the past. This trend can be stopped simply by reading to our children, talking with them, or playing with them. We are not suggesting parents embark on any kind of rigorous programs with their child(ren). That is, speaking is learned and practiced through play and everyday activities. It is not necessary to structure learning through the use of workbooks or other teaching resources. Support, encouragement, and a positive home environment provide children with the necessary activities for language to develop.

How we speak to our children is also important. For example, a school secretary recently shared this story. A student named Craig apparently cut one of his fingers with his scissors. When he approached the teacher to tell her what had happened, Craig was told to go to the office. When Craig arrived at the office, the school secretary asked him why he was there. Holding his cut finger, he admitted, "I don't know. I think I have a detention." We can imagine the scene clearly—a busy classroom with many children clamoring for attention. The teacher likely assumed the student would get the care he needed in the office. However, her tone conveyed a different message. Mixed messages can also happen in the midst of our busy home lives. Occasionally, stop and ask your child if she has understood your message the way you have intended. Children focus as much and sometimes more on how something is said than simply on what is said.

The way adults understand things and accept them may be understood and accepted quite differently by children. For instance, a young friend, John-Paul, took one look at the table set with soup and grilled-cheese sandwiches and stomped away in anger. His mother asked him what was wrong and he answered, "It's not fair! How come we never have boy-cheese sandwiches?"

Tips for Talking to Babies and Toddlers

 Slow down your own speech when talking to children.

 Talk out loud about what you are doing or what your child is doing.

 After speaking, even with a baby, stop and let her answer. This is how children learn "turn-taking" in conversation.

Chapter Fourteen: Daily Activities to Encourage Speech Development

All parents expect their children will learn to speak. We don't worry, will they or won't they?

All parents expect their children will learn to speak. We don't worry whether they will or not. It is an assumption parents make unless they are aware of any physical disabilities. Parents' expectations affect speech development. If we showed that same kind of expectation in our children's abilities to learn to read and write, would they develop those skills as easily and as effortlessly? We believe they would. There are some family activities that can support children as they learn to speak. Many of these activities cost nothing but time. They build on what you are already doing at home and they can be fun for both children and adults! The following provide opportunities for children to explore, learn, and play with language.

Dress-up

Speech seems to be an inevitable part of dress-up play.

Speech seems to be an inevitable part of dress-up play. If you haven't already done so, you might start a dress-up box. A grocery box is sufficient or even an old suitcase—nothing fancy is required. Old clothes, donated by you or members of your family can be added as they are found. Items from second-hand stores, jewelry, or accessories add to the fun. Even old sheets make wonderful capes for the imaginative child. Children, playing alone or with friends and

Playing dress-up

brothers and sisters will use language in interesting and inventive ways because of the costumes and props they have to play with. While not every dress-up time will lead to a performance, many do develop into delightful impromptu plays.

Telephones, Tape Recorders, and Microphones

These kinds of toys provide children with endless opportunities to talk to themselves, to others, or to make-believe characters. Through their play, they learn how to have conversations. You will have observed how differently your child speaks depending on whether she is talking to an adult or to another child. For instance, your child learns quickly to speak one way in the doctor's office and another way at home with brothers and sisters.

A microphone might be used for singing and dancing, interviewing or reporting. Children who are somewhat quiet or reserved often come alive or at least become excited about talking if they can use a microphone or tape recorder. Lisa's oldest son was fascinated by the announcer's voice on the weather channel. Perhaps it had a soothing quality. As a result, the family was treated to months of Jesse's weathercasts broadcast through a plastic microphone he carried with him everywhere.

Tape recorders can provide a different kind of experience. Children love to experiment with their own voices. Most can't wait to hear how they sound. Favorite stories and music can be played over and over again and this also contributes to language development. It is amazing how quickly children can memorize stories and musical selections by listening to a tape recording and practicing on their own. Parents, when reading to children, can also record themselves so that their children can play back favorite stories on their own.

Children use these props for their play because they have watched others (parents, siblings, and friends) use these items for a purpose. We often chuckle while watching a young child speak into a toy telephone. The child speaks, then pauses as if listening to someone else speak. She knows about talking on the phone because she has observed you and is trying to be like you by imitating your actions.

Puppets and Other Props

All children find favorite playthings—a stuffed bear, a baby doll, or even a soft blanket. These items accompany them wherever they go and it is not long before objects are given lifelike qualities. Dad says, "Are you looking for Winnie the Pooh? Where is he? Let's look for Pooh bear together! Here he is. He was hiding behind the chair." Children talk to these favored items, caress them, take care of them, get frustrated with them, and love them. As they grow older, their talk becomes more complex. They may use their toys to act out stories like, "Hansel and Gretel" or "Red Riding Hood."

> **What is interesting about children's language,... is that even though they may be retelling a familiar story, they are using their own words.**

What is interesting about children's language, especially during playtime, is that even though they may be retelling a familiar story, they are using their own words. They do not learn to speak simply by imitating others. Rather, they are able to hear words and then reinvent the language for themselves. They do this so that they can make sense of the world around them.

Using toys to tell stories

Books and Stories

Have you ever watched a three- or four-year-old turn the pages of a book, look at the pictures, and tell the story without reading a single word? Such activities allow children to use and practice language while doing what comes naturally—playing! This is a normal activity and it is important to respond, "Wow, you are a great reader!" This is especially true for toddlers and preschoolers who won't know the difference between real reading and pretend reading. When David's daughter, Stacey, then aged three, looked at pictures from a Mother Goose Nursery Rhyme book, she was able to recite entire nursery rhymes. At first her parents thought she was really reading each page. Later, it was discovered she was using clues from the pictures to "read" the rhymes.

As children grow older, talk with them about the books the two of you share together. It is important to discuss ideas and stories that interest your child. One book that many children love is *Strega Nona* by Tomie dePaola. If your son or daughter says, "I know where Strega Nona went. She went to town. Then you can reply, "How do you know?" This type of question helps the conversation between the two of you to go further. Whereas, if you say, "Oh I don't think so!" or "You're right," notice that the conversation stops.

Recently a parent shared with us her personal frustration with reading to her son. He constantly interrupted the reading of a story to talk. He wanted to talk about the story, the characters, the pictures, what would happen next, what had just happened or how the story would turn out. When we suggested that his own questions and comments were to be encouraged, she appeared relieved but still frustrated. It seems it often took a long time to get through a book. In such cases, it might be better to tell your child you can:

- read the whole story and then talk about it (particularly if other children are present), or
- talk as we go along, or
- pause after each page.

This way, you both have some expectations about what will happen during story time. However, it is always a good idea to encourage discussion about stories!

Questions and More Questions

Children ask many questions.

Children, thankfully, ask many questions. "What's that? Where did it go? Who's there? When can we go? and Why? Why? Why?" At about twenty months of age children begin asking **what**, **where**, and **who** questions. These questions are less abstract than **why**, **when**, or **how** questions and when you answer them, you can usually point to or show them the answer. Sometimes what a child is asking can be confusing. For instance, pointing to a person, a two-year-old might ask, "What's that?" instead of, "Who's that?" In this case it is important to understand the context of the child's question to know how to answer it.

Children do not generally ask questions to be bothersome or demanding. Through questioning they are developing an understanding of their world. Later, after the age of two, they will ask **why**, **when**, and **how**. Naturally, these questions require more abstract answers. For example, your child may say, "When are we going to Grandma's?" You respond, "Tomorrow." Tomorrow, as we all know, never comes and cannot really be understood as an object that the child can see or feel. Therefore, the child has asked the question but may not understand the answer until you say something like, "After one sleep!" Suddenly, your child is satisfied with your response. This is because you

have made an abstract idea like "tomorrow" understandable for the child. Although children's questioning can seem to be never ending, we are challenged to respond to them and keep responding until we have found the way to satisfy their insatiable curiosity!

Daily Activities to Encourage Speech Development

 Dress-up

 Telephones, tape recorders, and microphones

 Puppets and other props

 Books and stories

 Questions

Conversation Starters

What about your questions? As children become more able to carry on a conversation with you, adopt the technique of asking questions that encourage children to tell or explain a story, an activity, or event. Try some of the following ideas.

1. After your child has been on an outing, such as a school field-trip or a birthday party, ask him to tell you about it. Try asking, "What was your favorite part? What was the funniest thing that happened? Would our family like to go there? Why?"

2. It is also helpful to have your children describe something or someone to you. Remember, your questions have to be honest ones, not questions you already know the answers to. Otherwise your child will know you are just quizzing him and not really engaging in a conversation.

   Not long ago, Robin asked her daughter and her friend to describe a game they had played at a birthday party. Together they talked, used hand gestures, interrupted each other, spoke at the same time, asked one another questions, and contradicted each other until they finally finished the explanation. Until Robin asked them the question, they knew, in their own minds, how the game had been played. It was only in talking about it out loud that they were able to show their knowledge not only to a listener but to themselves as well. In the group telling, each friend could also clear up any inconsistencies in how they understood the game.

3. Another type of question to use, when the situation arises, is "what if ...?" A question like this encourages your child to think about possibilities, to problem-solve and then to make a choice. One example of this might occur when you and your child(ren) are baking or cooking together. You might say, "what would happen if we didn't add any baking soda to the dough?" An older child who knows what baking soda does when it is added to the ingredients, can offer a possible explanation. "What if ...?" questions can be asked at any time depending upon the situation—in the garage, watering the lawn, repairing a car, cooking, on a trip, wherever you find yourselves.

It is possible to see how, by building on what families do, parents and caregivers can help support the development of their children's speaking skills.

Conversation Starter Hints

📖 After an outing, ask your child questions such as, "What did you enjoy most?" Show genuine interest in her answers.

📖 Have your child describe someone they know to you (a favorite teacher, a new friend, or a coach) or something that has happened.

📖 Ask, "What if …? questions during reading or other activities to help your child use language to make predictions and to consider many possibilities about the book or the event.

Chapter Fifteen: What the Teacher Does and Why

Those of you who have children in school may notice that many report cards have sections devoted to listening skills and speaking skills. You may have wondered what the teacher is looking for in these two areas. This is a difficult question because different teachers will likely stress different things in regard to listening and speaking. However, it is most likely that your child's teacher is interested in both the *informal* and the *structured* aspect of these two skills.

Informal Listening and Speaking Skills

When children enter grade one, parents and teachers have certain expectations about how they should listen to and speak with others.

When children enter grade one, parents and teachers have certain expectations about how they should listen to and speak with others. Certainly these two skills will develop over the course of a school year and, therefore, children should not be expected to have mastered them within the first few weeks of school.

Children speak and listen in informal situations throughout the day. These include listening and speaking with brothers, sisters, friends, and family, as well as any other interactions that are spontaneous and unrehearsed. For example, your child hears your directions upon waking. You ask her to get dressed, make the bed, and eat breakfast. As you speak to your child, she senses your tone of voice, your body language, and other unspoken (nonverbal) messages in order to help her understand what you wish to communicate. In other words, your child does much more than simply hear what you say.

Informal speaking situations

How well your child learns to interpret all the signals sent to her will influence how effective a listener she will become. Speaking skills will also be influenced. As she interacts with family, friends, and peers, she will change her tone of voice, volume, and inflections in order to communicate effectively.

In school, your child's teacher carefully observes how well your child is able to listen and speak in these informal situations. For example, our own children have received suggestions like, "Timothy needs to spend less time talking with his friends in school," and "Ashley should practice speaking up in class more." Each of these comments reflects the teacher's classroom expectations with regards to listening and speaking. The first step is to talk with the teacher to clarify these comments so that you are able to help your child at home with specific behaviors that will carry over to school listening and speaking skills. In the first case, Timothy is being asked to concentrate more on school work during class time. In the second, Ashley is being encouraged to participate more in class discussions. Comments such as these remind us that we need to provide specific positive suggestions and guidance to help children in the situations in which they find themselves. Too often we have assumed that our children know how to listen and speak effectively in informal situations.

What You Can Do

Homes have become inundated with "noise" from so many sources. TV, radio, stereo, telephone, or computer can make it difficult for your child to concentrate on spoken messages. In fact, many children grow up in a kind of agitated state, unable to concentrate deeply for any length of time. For this reason, many parents limit their children's use of electronic equipment. It can be a good idea to set limits. Some families limit TV viewing to one hour on a school day. Other parents unplug the telephone during mealtimes or after a certain time in the evening. Some parents have children turn off video or computer games when they speak to them. Children learn to select only those shows they really want to watch or games they find enjoyable when there are limits in place.

Computers have their place.

> **Be aware that home can be a place to "wind down" after a busy and hectic day. Home can also be a place to develop listening and speaking skills in a relaxed atmosphere.**

These suggestions may help to eliminate some of the noise that makes it difficult for your child to concentrate on more than one message at a time (including yours!) and to filter out the important messages. Be aware that home can be a place to "wind down" after a busy and hectic day. Home can also be a place to the develop listening and speaking skills in a relaxed atmosphere.

Social Language

Some children might need help to become effective listeners and speakers. For example, you may notice that your child seems to ignore his playmates' (or an adult's) requests. He may have heard the request but thinks that by not responding, he is communicating that his answer is, "I don't want to give it to you." It is quite acceptable to talk to your child about good listening manners in informal situations. You might talk about eye contact, that is, having your child look at the person to whom he is listening. Many children react with either a nod "yes" or a shake "no" but often do not explain their responses. You could explain that it is helpful when someone is asking him a question, to answer it by using words. You may be thinking, "That's not my child! He's never quiet and he doesn't need to be reminded to speak up!" However, in these informal listening and speaking situations, some children do need help in learning how to speak and listen with confidence.

Young children often need help from you to solve a problem. Perhaps he is having difficulty getting along with a friend. If you watch what is happening, you may find that your child (or perhaps the other child) needs some help learning to express himself using the right words. Even with the right words two children will argue over a toy, but without words there can be no satisfactory resolution.

> **One great way to help your child solve a problem is to role-play a situation together.**

One great way to help your child solve a problem is to role-play a situation together. For example, if your child comes home from school and tells you that he is having trouble seeing the board, suggest that you be the teacher and have him practice telling you the problem. By doing this, you are helping him to see that he can handle a problem on his own and you are showing him (modeling) how to express himself effectively.

Structured Listening and Speaking Skills

Some examples of structured school-related speaking activities include practicing and performing a story or a play, making announcements, reading one's own stories or reports, conducting an interview, leading discussions, and asking and answering questions. Structured listening may include watching a film or video presentation to answer specific questions. It includes gaining specific information, listening to a guest speaker, participating in a group project, listening to a musical selection for mood or rhythm, or hearing a story read aloud in order to identify the main idea or other details. Generally, structured listening and speaking involve some form of practice.

To find out how well children speak and listen in these structured situations, teachers may administer speaking or listening tests at regular intervals throughout the school year. It is not uncommon for children to do well on informal listening and speaking activities but have trouble with the more structured aspect. When you speak with the teacher about your child's listening and speaking habits, ask how structured or informal situations are handled in the class. Knowing this will help you know how best to help your child.

Classroom Expectations

Speaking in a classroom is different from speaking at home.

One of the most difficult aspects of beginning school for many children is related to the new structure of speaking. Speaking in a classroom is different from speaking at home. Classroom expectations serve to introduce and practice structured listening and speaking skills. As preschoolers, most children speak whenever they choose and about whatever interests them. In kindergarten and grade one, however, it is estimated that more than 80% of their day is devoted to listening. In addition, speaking occurs according to a new set of rules. "Raise your hand *before* speaking, speak one at a time, and use only a quiet voice."

What You Can Do

> **In some classrooms much of the talk is directed to the teacher and this is frustrating to a child who has, up until this point, spoken freely to those around her.**

In some classrooms much of the talk is directed to the teacher and this is frustrating to a child who has, up until this point, spoken freely to those around her. Studies of babies' learning abilities show that those early "conversations" between parents and children really do set the groundwork for later language development. If you sense your child is having difficulty in this area, it would be a good idea to call the teacher and ask how much time is spent on structured and on informal listening and speaking activities. If possible, try to gradually introduce your child to structured listening and speaking situations over the first year of schooling so that the classroom expectations are not too severe. This can be done through parent and child play groups, nursery and preschool experiences, and story time at the library, just to name a few. By talking with your child's teacher and sharing information about your child's speaking and listening habits outside school, you may be able to help bridge the home experience and the school experience in a way that supports your child's development.

Hints for Helping Children Develop Successful Speaking and Listening Skills

- Turn off the television, computer, and/or telephone in the evening (perhaps once a week) to help your child "wind down" from a hectic day.

- Role-play life situations with your child so that she can practice listening and speaking to others in what may be stressful situations, for example, when someone hurts her feelings.

- Talk with the teacher about your child's listening and speaking habits in school to see if you both view your child in the same way.

Chapter Sixteen: What You May Be Concerned About (Questions and Answers)

 My four-year-old says, "I don't got none!" I take the time to tell him that it's not right and get him to repeat me, "I don't have any." He *can* say it correctly but he doesn't. How come?

Learning language is a developmental process which means that children must go through certain stages as they become proficient users of language. Interestingly, teaching children certain aspects of the language, like you are trying to do, doesn't really speed up the process. Right now, your son has learned to use negatives in his speech. In doing this, he uses lots of negatives in each utterance. It will take time for him to use "standard" negatives. In the meantime, he is practicing or possibly over-practicing what he has learned. By using standard speech yourself like, "That's right, Timmy, you don't have any," you are giving him as much help as he needs in this stage of his development.

 Can a child ever talk too much? Our daughter never seems to be quiet except when she's sleeping!

 Once children learn to talk, it can seem like too much of a good thing! While it may be frustrating for you particularly if you're trying to have a conversation with someone else, it is still important to respond to your child's questions and comments. An interesting characteristic about children learning to talk is that most young children initiate all the conversations between you and them. And because you respond with interest, they are reinforced to continue. If you consider it, there are very few times in their lives (except in learning to talk) that they can initiate an activity. That is, we decide when it's time to eat, sleep, play, go for a drive, and visit Grandma. Yet learning to speak always begins with the child. Therefore, it is quite important to respond to them as they make such initiations. Of course, as they get older, you may set some rules like, "Please don't interrupt me when I'm speaking to someone else unless it's an emergency."

Q: My friend's five-year-old son speaks much more clearly than my own and he uses harder vocabulary too! Have we done something wrong? Does he need to be tested?

A: Remember that each child follows his or her own set of developmental stages. Not all children will (or should) be at the same stage at the same time. Try not to compare your child's development to that of his friends, particularly in front of him. This could cause him to doubt himself and slow his development for the time being. If you are very concerned, however, and have trouble yourself understanding your son, you may wish to discuss your concerns (in private) with your family doctor, pediatrician, or health-care professional. In the meantime, continue to model good speaking habits. Slow down your speech just a bit and pronounce words carefully when speaking to your son, in case he is imitating your own "fast-talking" habit.

Q: I'm worried because I seem to be the only person who knows what my two-and-one-half-year-old is saying. When will her language make sense to others?

A: Mothers and babies seem to have a language all their own. Researchers have actually called the conversations that occur between mothers and their infants, Motherese. Because you spend so much time with your child, you pick up on all her speech patterns. It doesn't take long before you recognize that your toddler wants some milk when she points to the fridge and says, "Ahhh?" As her language continues to develop, you are attuned to not only what she says but also how she says it. You watch for her facial expressions, her gestures, and her tone of voice to help you make sense of her utterances. And when you respond incorrectly, by giving her some milk when she really wanted a toy, she lets you know (perhaps by tossing the milk to the floor)! So, chances are, you've become an expert on reading the language signals your daughter sends. Naturally someone who doesn't know your child as well does not understand your child's utterances as readily. This isn't your child's fault or problem. A two-and-one-half-year-old has lots of time to develop easily recognizable speech patterns and should be encouraged to do so at her own rate.

My son who is in grade one speaks very quickly (and so do I) but at school, the teacher says she and his friends don't always understand him. What should we do?

 First, because you have said that speaking quickly is a speech pattern that you have, it will be important to modify *your* behavior in order to help your son. It is a matter of being conscious of your speech patterns and making a concentrated effort to slow down, especially when speaking with your son. Try to get your son to look at the person to whom he is speaking or listening as this can help others make sense of what he is saying. Using a mirror can also help. Take a few minutes, maybe after he brushes his teeth, and have your child watch his mouth as he practices certain phrases that are particularly difficult to understand like, "Watchadon," which is a version of, "What are you doing?" When he sees how his mouth is moving while he is speaking, he may become more conscious of his own speech. Do not go on and on about the "problem," as this can make a child feel inadequate about himself. Speak to his teacher for other ideas about supporting your child's speech development.

 I am not sure how to go about talking to my child's teacher about problems and concerns I might have. What do you suggest?

 First and most important, don't wait too long before calling the teacher about a particular concern. If something is bothering you or your child, then call the teacher right away. Most teachers want to know about problems, questions, and concerns as they arise. This is so that something can be done to address the situation before it becomes a big problem. Not every situation means you must have a face-to-face meeting; many questions can be discussed over the telephone.

Tell the teacher how your child thinks or feels about a particular problem and then ask the teacher for assistance. For example, if your child does not want to go to school because he is sitting by another child who is bothering him, explain that to the teacher and ask what can be done. Think of yourself and the teacher as partners who are trying to do the best for your child.

Finally, set a positive tone for conversations you have at home about school and about teachers. If you speak negatively about school experiences, then your children will learn to do the same. In this case it won't be long before they decide that school has little to offer them.

Q: Our daughter is six years old and is unable to make an L sound. It always comes out as an R sound in words *like*, *lost*, *yellow*, and *ball*. What should we do?

A: This is not uncommon. Something I tried with my daughter might work for you. First, I did not want to make my daughter feel as though something was wrong with her so I did not talk about it too often. Instead, I realized that since her favorite friend's name was **Lucy** which began with the letter **L**, I had an opportunity to talk with my daughter about the **L** sound. Whenever she said her friend's name, I would repeat, "Yes, Lucy! What letter does Lucy start with?" I over-stressed the **L** sound so she could hear it and watch how I made the sound with my tongue pushed against the back of my front teeth. Without making a big deal of her pronunciation, eventually she picked up the sound by becoming conscious of it in certain words. Remember even though your child has difficulty with one sound, there are many others she has learned correctly.

Q: My daughter Krista, who is four years old, doesn't ask *why* questions very often. Should I be worried or will she begin this soon? What if I'm not able to answer some of the questions?

A: First, remember that **why** questions usually come later because these are abstract questions for children to ask and to understand. The exception is the "why, why, why" syndrome that some, though not all, two-year-olds demonstrate. It seems they continually ask this because they want to see how far it will go and probably because it seems to frustrate you.

You may, at opportune moments, ask a **why** question of your own—not because you expect an answer but more because you are simply wondering out loud. For example, if you and your daughter are at the park and see a bird flying in and out of a tree, you might say, "I wonder why that bird is flying in and out of the tree so often?" Your child might offer an explanation if you do this consistently. If she doesn't, then you could answer your own question, "Maybe she's bringing food to her babies in a nest. What do you think?" Soon, wondering out loud will be something you both do when it seems appropriate. Unfortunately, some school experiences teach children only to answer rather than ask questions. If you make it a habit to wonder out loud, your child may continue to develop her question-asking abilities.

What if I am not able to understand McKenzie's questions?

As for not knowing how to respond all the time, don't worry because we've all been there. Sometimes a child's question is hard to answer because it deals with a sensitive issue or because we want to say "the right thing," or we simply don't know the answer. It's always a good idea to begin by telling your child how you feel about the question first. Try, "That's a hard question for me because...." or "What a great question. I don't know the answer. I wonder how we can find out." You can always tell your child that you'd like time to think about a question she has asked, saying you'll get back to her on it. This gives you time to think about how you could respond. You don't need to know the answers to everything that your child asks, but by showing her you are interested in her questions, you are telling her that she and her ideas are important to you!

Wrapping Up—
What We Have Learned

From Your Child's Teacher: Helping Your Child Learn to Read, Write, and Speak is designed to help parents feel both comfortable and competent as they develop ways to support their children's literacy development. Our message is that parents are, and will always be, a child's first and most important teachers. It is also important to acknowledge the role parents play, on a daily basis, in developing a child's literacy skills. Each section of this book provides ways to use the most natural of family activities to enhance a child's ability to read, write, and speak. Our stories, anecdotes, and suggestions demonstrate that parents can build upon pre-existing routines and activities to support learning from birth through to adolescence.

Parents and teachers have the same goal for their children. They want children to develop into successful readers, writers, and speakers so they can meet the future with confidence, success, and joy. To meet this goal, communication between the home and the school must be frequent. Stay informed about your child's progress, about the teacher's expectations and about your role in supporting your child's developing literacy skills. Above all, trust your own abilities as a parent to guide your child toward the future.

information at a glance

The materials included in this section are designed to help the reader view summaries of the book's content and information at a glance. Permission is given to reproduce these summaries in school and parent newsletters or to share with other parents, friends, and family.

Section Four: Information at a Glance

Appendix 1

When to Begin

Here are some things you can do to start the reading habit early.

- 📖 Start reading to your child today.

- 📖 Make sure your home contains lots of reading material—library books, magazines, newspapers, recipe books, notes, and messages posted on a bulletin board.

- 📖 Show your child that you read.

It's never too early.

Appendix 2

Helpful Reading Hints (Birth to Two Years)

Try these reading suggestions with your babies and toddlers.

- Sit comfortably with your child in your lap while you read aloud from a book and talk about the pictures.

- Offer your baby a magazine to look at in her high chair or play pen while you are cooking supper.

- Visit your local library to ensure a wide variety of books are in your home.

- Look at photograph albums with your child and tell the story of the event depicted in the photos.

Permission to reproduce

Appendix 3

Helpful Reading Hints (Ages Three to Six)

Preschoolers and children in the primary grades will benefit from some of the following reading strategies.

- When your child finishes reading a page whether it has been memorized or retold, say, "Wow, that was terrific! You really know that story. Let's go back and see if we can find all the words that begin like your name—Brianne."

- Try a reading game called, "I Start, You Finish." The parent begins the sentence or paragraph and then stops; the child continues.

- Use "tracking" by pointing to the words as you read them to show your child that the words you are saying are the words on the page. Eventually your child will take over this task.

Permission to reproduce

Appendix 4

Helpful Reading Hints (Ages Seven to Ten)

These reading strategies are helpful to beginning and developing readers who are just learning to think of themselves as real readers.

 Try the "My Turn, Your Turn" method. You read one paragraph, one chapter, or one page and then your child reads the next one.

 For a shy reader, use the "Fade In, Fade Out" approach. Begin by reading together. As you hear your child's voice getting stronger, fade out by lowering your voice. If your child struggles, fade in again and provide help.

 Try questioning techniques that help your child to think about the story. Questions that help children to think about stories include:

- How are you like the character in this story?
- What would you do if you were in the story?
- What does this story remind you of?

 Use lead-ins to encourage your child to talk about their thoughts while reading. Try saying, "I really liked the part when _____," and then let your child finish the phrase.

Permission to reproduce

Appendix 5

Helpful Reading Hints (Ages Eleven and Up)

Even when older children show that they can read independently, there are some ways parents can continue supporting their development as readers.

- Ask your child what she is learning about in other subject areas like social studies, science, and mathematics where reading is important to doing well.

- If your child struggles with reading textbooks at school, ask the teacher if you can have copies of these at home to read together.

- Encourage your child to read about topics that interest her even if it is not something being studied at school. For instance, find books in the library about motorcycles, dinosaurs, fighter planes, Egyptian mummies or anything else that interests your child.

- Help your child find books that are written just for adolescents about difficult issues such as sibling rivalry, death and dying, divorce, and challenges of adolescence.

Permission to reproduce

Appendix 6

Stuck on a Word? Steps to Help Your Child

If your child is reading to you and comes to an unfamiliar word:

1. Wait three or four seconds to see what she does. If this doesn't work, then go on to the next step.

2. Say, "Can you sound out the word?" Make the first sound(s) to get him started. If this doesn't work, then go on to the next step.

3. If she sounds out each letter but still doesn't know what the word is, then suggest she look at the picture. Does this help? If this doesn't work, then go on to the next step.

4. Read the sentence again and stop before the unfamiliar word. Does this help? If this doesn't work, then go on to the next step.

5. Skip that word and have the child continue reading. Does he figure it out by reading to the end of the sentence, paragraph or page?

6. If she still cannot read the word, then tell her what it is and explain why it was a difficult word. E.g., In **action** the **tion** is pronounced **shun**.

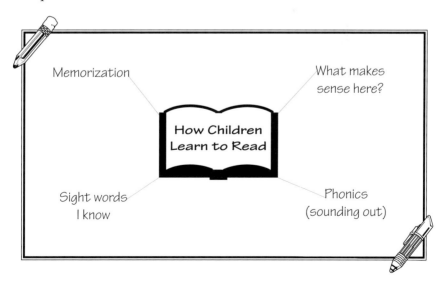

Permission to reproduce

Appendix 7

Stages of Writing Development

The following stages are used to describe the ways that children develop as writers. These stages are generally followed by children as they experiment with writing.

- **Playing on paper.** This is when children, generally toddlers, produce scribbles in the form of lines, dots, and circles.

- **Trying symbols.** Between three and five years of age, children try letters and numbers while writing. These are often first attempts at writing their own names or words they have seen around them.

- **Discovering letters.** Between three and six years of age children write letters that are meaningful to them. They write **m** for **mom** or perhaps learn to write all three letters.

- **Aha! Mommy starts with "m."** At this stage children recognize that letters and sounds go together. Examples of this kind of writing include, writing **u** for **you**, **lik** for **like**, or **sp** for **stop**.

- **Moving toward the "right way."** In the primary grades, children's writing develops into what teachers call "the standard version." Over time and with instruction, children learn to write **luv** as **love**. Typically, this is a long stage. It is not uncommon for some children to be using inventive spelling for some words into fifth or sixth grade.

Permission to reproduce

Appendix 8

Helping Children Develop As Writers

These strategies are useful to help children view writing as an important activity in their lives.

- Provide lots of different writing tools for your child to try.

- Display your child's art and writing around the house.

- Leave notes for your child to read.

- Comment on *what* your child has written before saying anything about *how* it is written.

- Point out words and letters in the environment—Stop and Yield signs, names of department and grocery stores, and places of interest in the neighborhood.

- Ask your child to tell you about his drawing or writing so you can see the thinking and ideas that contributed to his creation.

- Balance allowing children to sound out words for themselves and helping them with spelling when they ask for it.

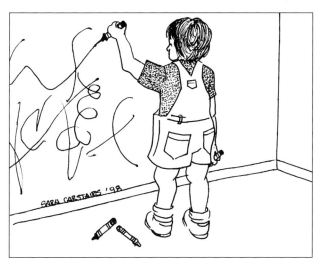

Permission to reproduce

Appendix 9

The Writing Process

As children progress through the elementary and junior high grades, they do more and more writing on their own. Students in schools mostly write using a series of steps teachers call **The Writing Process**. These steps are not used for every piece of writing a child produces. Rather, they are used as a guide to help children see how writers get started and how they eventually publish a piece.

1. **Prewriting.** Children are encouraged to decide on a writing topic.
2. **Drafting.** Children write their pieces focusing on the ideas they are writing about.
3. **Revising.** Children go back over their writing and rewrite parts to make their ideas clearer to a reader.
4. **Editing.** Children work on their writing to correct spelling, punctuation, and grammar.
5. **Publishing.** Children display their writing in some way so that it can be shared with others.

The diagram at the right shows one version of **The Writing Process.*** Note that many of the arrows are double-sided, meaning that many aspects of the process are not sequential steps, but rather are intertwined.

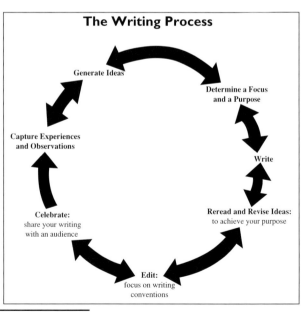

*Peterson, Shelley. (1995). *Becoming Better Writers.* Edmonton, AB: FP Hendriks Publishing Ltd.

Permission to reproduce

Appendix 10

Encouraging Daily Writing

Here are some daily activities you and your child can try to encourage writing.

 Calendar

Display a large calendar on the refrigerator or a bulletin board to write in special days, appointments, and other important activities.

 Playtime

Keep paper and writing materials out for your child to use when playing.

 Signs

Parents and children can leave notes for one another about phone calls, reminders, and other messages.

 Thank-You Notes

Together, parents and children can create thank-you notes for special people in their lives.

Permission to reproduce

Appendix 11

Daily Activities to Encourage Speech Development

Here are some family activities that support children as they learn to speak. They build on what you are already doing at home and they can be fun for both children and adults.

- **Dress-up.** Store dress-up clothes in a grocery box or an old suitcase. Children, playing alone or with friends and brothers and sisters, will use language in interesting and inventive ways because of the costumes and props they have to play with.

- **Telephones, Tape Recorders, and Microphones.** These kinds of toys provide children with endless opportunities to talk to themselves, to others, or to make-believe characters.

- **Puppets and Other Props.** All children find "favorite" playthings—a stuffed bear, a baby doll, or even a soft blanket. They may use these toys to have conversations, to act out stories, or to play.

- **Books and Stories.** Favorite stories can be shared and discussed together. Resist the temptation to "get through" a book. Instead, let your child talk about what is interesting to her while reading.

- **Questions.** Use your children's questions as opportunities to talk about their ideas, thoughts, and wonderings. Children's questions are seldom meant to be bothersome or demanding. Rather, their questions are important to developing an understanding of a variety of events in their lives.

Permission to reproduce

Appendix 12

Conversation Starter Hints

As children become able to carry on a conversation with you, adopt the technique of encouraging conversations that help children tell or explain a story, an activity, an event, or a person.

- After an outing, ask your child questions such as, "What did you enjoy most?" Show a genuine interest in your child's answers.

- Have your child describe someone they know to you (a favorite teacher, a new friend, or a coach) or event that has happened.

- Ask, "What if …?" questions during reading or other activity to help your child use language to make predictions and to consider many possibilities about the book or the event.

Permission to reproduce

Appendix 13

Books About Teaching Spelling

Bean, W. & Bouffler, C. (1987). *Spell by Writing*. Rozelle, NSW: Primary English Teaching Association.

Gentry, J.R. (1987). *Spel ... is a Four-Letter Word*. Portsmouth, NII: Heinemann.

Grambs, D. (1992). *The Ultimate Spelling Quiz Book*. New Jersey: Random House.

Morris, Thea R. (1994). *Making Spelling Fun! Ideas that Work*. Calgary, AB: Jellybean Connections.

Read, C. (1986). *Children's Creative Spelling*. London: Routledge & Kegan Paul.

Tarasoff, M. (1992). *A Guide to Children's Spelling Development: For Parents and Teachers*. Victoria, BC: Activity Learning Institute.

Tarasoff, M. (1990). *Spelling: Strategies You Can Teach*. Victoria, BC: Pixelart Graphics.

Wilde, S. (1993). *You Kan Red This! Spelling and Punctuation for Whole Language Classrooms, K-6*. Portsmouth, NH: Heinemann.

Permission to reproduce

Appendix 14

Professional References

Atwell, N. (1999). *In the Middle: Writing, Reading, and Learning with Adolescents* (2nd Ed.). Portsmouth, NH: Heinemann.

Bright, R. (1995). *Writing Instruction in the Intermediate Grades: What is Said, What is Done, What is Understood.* Newark, DE: International Reading Assocation.

Dahl, K & Farnon, N. (1998). *Children's Writing: Perspectives from Research.* Newark, DE: International Reading Association.

Gleason, J. (1997). *The Development of Language.* Needham Heights, MA: Allyn & Bacon.

Hulit, L. & Howard, M. (1997). *Born to Talk: An Introduction to Speech and Language Development.* Needham Heights, MA: Allyn & Bacon.

Graves, D. (1988). *Writing: Teachers and Children at Work.* Portsmouth, NH: Heinemann.

McGee, L. (1998). "How Do We Teach Literature to Young Children?" In S. Neuman & K. Roskos (Eds.) *Children Achieving: Best Practices in Early Literacy.* Newark, DE: International Reading Association.

Newman, S. & Roskos, K. (1998). *Children Achieving: Best Practices in Early Literacy.* Newark, DE: International Reading Association.

Peterson, S. (1995). *Becoming Better Writers.* Edmonton, AB: FP Hendriks Publishing.

Power, B. (1999). *Parent Power: Energizing Home-School Communication.* Portsmouth, NH: Heinemann.

Short, K., Harste, J. & Burke, C. (1996). *Creating Classrooms for Authors and Inquirers* (2nd ed.). Portsmouth, NH: Heinemann.

Stewig, J. & Jett-Simpson, M. (1995) *Language Arts in the Early Childhood Classroom.* Scarborough, ON: Wadsworth Publishing Co.

Permission to reproduce

Stoll, D. (1998). *Magazines for Kids and Teens*. Newark, DE: International Reading Association.

Tompkins, G., Bright, R., Pollard, M., & Winsor, P. (1999). *Language Arts: Content and Teaching Strategies*. Scarborough, ON: Prentice-Hall.

Wells, G. (1986). *The Meaning Makers: Children Learning Language and Using Language to Learn*. Portsmouth, NH: Heinemann.

Zola, M (1998). "Passing on the Words." *Orbit*. Vol. 28, No. 4, pp. 30–33. Toronto, ON: University of Toronto Press.

book lists for children and young adults

This section contains book lists for children from very young to pre-teen. Permission is given to reproduce these lists to include in newsletters or to share with other parents, friends, and family.

Section Five: Book Lists for Children and Young Adults

Birth to Two Years

Alphabet, Counting, and Discovering the World Books

Ahlberg, J. & Ahlberg, A. (1979). *Peek-a-Boo!* [illus by authors]. New York: Viking Press.

Alderson, Sue Ann. (1993). *A Ride For Martha* [illus by Ann Blades]. Toronto, ON: Douglas & McIntyre.

Allen, J. (1992). *One with a Bun.* New York: Morrow.

Base, Graeme. *Anamalia.* (1987). Richmond Hill, ON: Irwin.

Dragonwagon, Crescent. (1987). *Alligator Arrived with Apples: A Potluck Alphabet Feast* [illus by Jose Aruego and Ariane Dwey]. New York: Macmillan.

Ehlert, Lois. (1989). *Eating the Alphabet: Fruits and Vegetables from A to Z* [illus by author]. Toronto, ON: Harcourt Brace &Co.

Hill, Eric. (1989). *Spot Counts from 1 to 10* [illus by author]. [Series: Little Spot Board Books]. New York: Putnam.

Hill, Eric. (1986). *Spot Looks at Colors* [illus by author]. New York: Putnam.

Hoban, Tana. (1989). *Of Colors and Things.* New York: Greenwillow.

Hoban, Tana. (1984). *Is it Rough? Is it Smooth? Is it Shiny?* [illus by author]. New York: Greenwillow.

Hughes, Shirley. (1986). *Colors* [illus by author]. New York: Lothrop.

Hughes, Shirley. (1985). *When We Went to the Park* [illus by author]. New York: Lothrop.

Jonas, Ann. (1984). *Holes and Peeks* [illus by author]. New York: Greenwillow.

Little, Lessie Jones & Eloise Greenfield. (1978). *I Can Do It by Myself* [illus by Carole Byard]. New York: Harper.

Martin, Bill Jr. & John Archambault. (1989). *Chicka Chicka Boom Boom* [illus by Lois Ehlert]. Torrance, CA: Simon & Schuster.

Permission to reproduce

Oxenbury, Helen. (1987). *Clap Hands*. Vancouver, BC: Douglas & McIntyre.

Tafuri, Nancy. (1987). *Where We Sleep* [illus by author]. New York: Greenwillow.

Viorst, Judith. (1994). *The Alphabet from Z to A: With Much Confusion on the Way*. Indianapolis, IN: Macmillan.

Bedtime Books

Apple, Margot. (1990). *Blanket* [illus]. Boston: Houghton.

Brown, Margaret Wise. (1947). *Goodnight Moon* [illus by Clement Hurd]. New York: Harper LB.

Bunting, Eve. (1989). *No Nap* [illus by Susan Meddaugh]. Boston: Houghton Mifflin.

Carlstrom, Nancy White. (1992). *Northern Lullaby* [illus by Diane Dillon & Leo Dillon]. New York: Putnam.

Emberley, Ed. (1993). *Go Away, Big Green Monster!* Boston: Little, Brown.

Ginsburg, Mirra. (1992). *Asleep, Asleep* [illus by Nancy Tafuri]. New York: Greenwillow.

Johnson, Ryerson. (1989). *Why is Baby Crying?* [illus by DyAnne DiSalvo-Ryan]. Niles, IL: Whitman.

Lipniacka, Ewa. (1991). *To Bed ... or Else!* [illus by Basia Bogdanowicz]. New York: Crocodile.

Loh, Morag. (1988). *Tucking Mommy In* [illus by Donna Tawlins]. New York: Orchard.

McGilvray, Richard. (1993). *Don't Climb Out of the Window Tonight* [illus by Alan Snow]. New York: Dial.

Mayer, Mercer. (1987). *There's An Alligator under My Bed* [illus by author]. New York: Dial.

Morris, Winifred. (1990). *What If the Shark Wears Tennis Shoes?* [Illus by Betsy Levin]. New York: Atheneum.

Oxenbury, Helen. (1987). *Say Goodnight* [illus by author]. Vancouver, BC: Douglas & McIntyre.

Zolotow, Charlotte. (1991). *The Summer Night* [illus by Ben Schecter]. New York: Harper.

Permission to reproduce

Nursery Rhymes

Chorao, Kay. (1986). *The Baby's Good Morning Book* [illus by author]. New York: Dutton.

Hale, Sara Josepha. (1990). *Mary Had a Little Lamb* [illus by Bruce McMillan]. New York: Scholastic.

Hayes, Sarah. (1988). *Clap Your Hands: Finger Rhymes* [illus by Toni Goffe]. New York: Lothrop.

Lottridge, Celia (ed.). (1994). *Mother Goose: A Canadian Sampler* [illus by Canadian illustrators]. Toronto, ON: Groundwood.

Mother Goose. (1993). *The House That Jack Built* [illus by Emily Bolam]. New York: Dutton.

Mother Goose. (1990). *The Baby's Lap Book* [illus by Kay Chorao]. New York: Dutton.

Stories Without Words

Blades, Ann. (1990). *Fall* [illus by author]. New York: Lothrop.

Brown, Craig. (1989). *The Patchwork Farmer* [illus]. New York: Greenwillow.

Cristini, Ermanno & Luigi Pericelli. (1984). *In the Pond* [illus by authors]. Natick, MA: Alphabet Press.

Goodall, John S. (1991). *Paddy Under Water* [illus by author]. San Diego: Harcourt.

Hughes, Shirley. (1986). *Up and Up* [illus by author]. New York: Lothrop.

Imershein, Betsy. (1989). *Finding Red Finding Yellow* [illus]. San Diego: Harcourt.

Krahn, Fernando. (1985). *Amanda & the Mysterious Carpet* [illus by author]. Boston: Houghton.

McCully, Emily Arnold. (1988). *The Christmas Gift* [illus by author]. New York: Harper.

Mayer, Mercer. (1967). *A Boy, A Dog and A Frog* [illus by author]. New York: Dial.

Ormerod, Jan. (1982). *Moonlight* [illus by author]. New York: Lothrop.

Permission to reproduce

Oxenbury, Helen. (1981). *Dressing* [illus by author]. New York: Simon & Schuster.

Reid, Barbara. (1991). *Zoe's Rainy Day* [illus by author]. Toronto, ON: Harper Collins.

Tafuri, Nancy. (1988). *Junglewalk* [illus by author]. New York: Greenwillow.

Picture Books

Ahlberg, Janet & Allan Ahlberg. (1995). *Bye Bye Baby: A Sad Story with a Happy Ending* [illus]. Boston: Little.

Allen, Judy. (1993). *Whale* [illus by Tudor Humphries]. Cambridge, MA: Candlewick.

Arnold, Tedd. (1987). *No Jumping on the Bed!* [illus by author]. New York: Dial.

Bang, Molly. (1985). *The Paper Crane.* New York: Greenwillow.

Baumgart, Klaus. (1992). *Anna and the Little Green Dragon* [illus by author]. New York: Hyperion.

Bogart, Jo Ellen. (1992). *Daniel's Dog* [illus by Janet Wilson]. Toronto, ON: Scholastic.

Calhoun, Mary. (1987). *Jack and the Whoopee Wind* [illus by Dick Gackenbach]. New York: Morrow.

Cole, Brock. (1991). *Alpha and the Dirty Baby* [illus]. New York: Farrar.

Coombs, Patricia. (1992). *Dorrie and the Haunted Schoolhouse.* Boston: Houghton.

Crewes, Donald. (1992). *Freight Train.* New York: Greenwillow.

Denton, Terry. (1990). *The School For Laughter* [illus]. Boston: Houghton.

Dijs, Carla. (1992). *Pretend You're a Hippo* [illus by author]. New York: Simon & Schuster.

Gackenbach, Dick. (1979). *Harry & the Terrible Whatzit* [illus by author]. Boston: Houghton.

Gifaldi, David. (1993). *The Boy Who Spoke Colors* [illus by C. Shana Greger]. Boston: Houghton.

Permission to reproduce

Hasler, Eveline. (1985). *Winter Magic* [illus by Michele Lemieux]. New York: Morrow.

Hines, Anna Grossnickle. (1992). *Moon's Wish* [illus]. Boston: Houghton.

Hoban, Russell. (1990). *Monsters* [illus by Quentin Blake]. New York: Scholastic.

Jackson, Ellen. (1991). *Ants Can't Dance* [illus by Frank Remkiewicz]. New York: Macmillan.

Lester, Helen. (1990). *Pookins Gets Her Way* [illus by Lynn Munsinger]. Boston: Houghton.

Macdonald, Maryann. (1991). *Sam's Worries* [illus by Judith Riches]. New York: Hyperion.

Mahy, Margaret. (1992). *The Dragon of an Ordinary Family* [illus by Helen Oxenbury]. Toronto, ON: Doubleday.

Naylor, Phyllis Reynolds. (1992). *The Boy With the Helium Head* [illus by Kay Chorao]. New York: Dell.

Pearson, Susan. (1990). *Well I Never!* [illus by James Warhola]. New York: Simon & Schuster.

Pittman, Helena Clare. (1988). *Once When I Was Scared* [illus by Ted Rand]. New York: Dutton.

Seuss, Dr. (1949). *Bartholomew & the Oobleck* [illus by author]. New York: Random.

Stanley, Diane. (1985). *Birdsong Lullaby* [illus by author]. New York: Morrow.

Stevenson, James. (1992). *Rolling Rose* [illus]. New York: Greenwillow.

Stinson, Kathy. (1982). *Red is Best*. Toronto, ON: Annick.

Tibo, Giles. (1991). *Simon & the Snowflakes* [illus]. Montreal, PQ: Tundra.

Westcott, Nadine Bernard. (1981). *The Giant Vegetable Garden* [illus by author]. Boston: Little, Brown.

Winthrop, Elizabeth. (1991). *A Very Noisy Girl* [illus by Ellen Weiss]. New York: Holiday.

Permission to reproduce

Ages Three to Six

Agard, John. (1989). *The Calypso Alphabet* [illus by Jennifer Bent]. New York: Henry Holt.

Anno, Mitsumasa. (1995). *Anno's Magic Seeds*. New York: Putnam/Philomel.

Anno, Mitsumasa. (1975). *Anno's Alphabet: An Adventure in Imagination* [illus by author]. New York: Harper.

Aruego, Jose. (1971). *Look What I Can Do!* [illus by author]. New York: Macmillan.

Baker, Kent. (1992). *Finster Frets* [illus by H. Werner Zimmerman]. Toronto, ON: Oxford University Press.

Balian, Lorna. (1992). *Humbug Witch* [illus by author]. New York: Humbug.

Bang, Molly. (1985). *The Paper Crane*. New York: Greenwillow.

Bang, Molly. (1983). *Ten, Nine, Eight* [illus by author]. New York: Greenwillow.

Bannatyne-Cugnet, Jo. (1994). *A Prairie Year* [illus by Yvette Moore]. Montreal, PQ: Tundra Books.

Calhoun, Mary. (1987). *Jack and the Whoopee Wind* [illus by Dick Gackenbach]. New York: Morrow.

Carle, Eric. (1981). *The Very Hungry Caterpillar* [illus by author]. New York: Putnam.

Crease, Skid (1994). *In the Great Meadow* [illus by Jan Thornhill]. Toronto, ON: Annick.

Crews, Donald. (1994). *Sail Away.* [illus]. New York: Greenwillow.

Crews, Donald. (1982). *Carousel* [illus by author]. New York: Greenwillow.

Crews, Donald. (1980). *Light* [illus]. New York: Greenwillow.

Cuyler Margery. (1992). *That's Good, That's Bad* [illus by David Catrow]. New York: Holt.

De Paola, Tomie. (1997). *Strega Nona*. New York: Simon & Schuster.

Donnelly, Liza. (1991). *Dinosaur Beach* [illus by author]. New York: Scholastic.

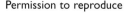
Permission to reproduce

Edwards, Frank B. (1995). *Mortimer Mooner Makes Lunch* [illus by John Bianchi]. Newburgh: Bungalo Books.

Ehlert, Lois. (1992). *Nuts to You* [illus]. San Diego: Harcourt.

Ehlert, Lois. (1990). *Feathers for Lunch.* San Diego: Harcourt.

Emberley, Barbara. (1972). *Drummer Hoff* [illus by Ed Emberley]. Richmond Hill, ON: Distican.

Ferber, Elizabeth. (1995). *The Squeeze-More-Inn* [illus by author]. Richmond Hill, ON: Scholastic.

Fitch, Sheree (1995). *I Am Small* [illus by Kim Lafave]. Toronto, ON: Doubleday.

Fox, Mem. (1989). *Koala Lou* [illus by Pamela Lofts]. New York: Harcourt.

Fox, Mem. (1986). *Hattie and the Fox* [illus by Patricia Mullins]. New York: Simon & Schuster.

French, Vivian. (1994). *Lazy Jack* [illus by Russell Ayto]. Cambridge, MA: Candlewick.

Galdone, Paul. (1974). *The Gingerbread Boy* [illus by author]. New York: Houghton Mifflin.

Giganti, Paul Jr. (1992). *Each Orange Had Eight Slices* [illus by Donald Crews]. New York: Greenwillow.

Gilman, Phoebe. (1995). *The Gypsy Princess.* Toronto, ON: Scholastic.

Ginsburg, Mirra (1974). *The Chick and the Duckling* [illus by Jose Aruego & Ariane Dewey]. New York: Simon and Schuster.

Gray, Libba Moore. (1994). *My Mama Had a Dancing Heart* [illus by Raúl Colón]. New York: Orchard/Melanie Kroupa.

Greaves, Margaret (1992). *Henry's Wild Morning* [illus by Teresa O'Brien]. New York: Dial.

Harrison, Ted. (1989). *A Northern Alphabet: A is for Arctic* [illus by author]. Montreal, PQ: Tundra.

Harrison, Troon. (1993). *The Long Weekend.* [illus by Michael Foreman]. Boston: Little, Brown.

Hearn, Diane Dawson. (1994). *Dad's Dinosaur Day* [illus by author]. New York: Macmillan.

Permission to reproduce

From Your Child's Teacher

Heller, Nicholas. (1991). *The Tooth Tree*. New York: Greenwillow.

Hines, Anna Grossnickle. (1992). *Rumbler Thumble Boom!* New York: Greenwillow.

Hoban, Tana. (1987). *26 Letters and 99 Cents* [illus by author]. New York: Greenwillow.

Hoban, Tana. (1978). *Is it Red? Is it Yellow? Is it Blue?* [illus]. New York: Greenwillow.

Hutchins, Pat. (1992). *The Wind Blew* [illus by author]. New York: Simon & Schuster.

Hutchins, Pat. (1985). *The Very Worst Monster* [illus by author]. New York: Greenwillow.

Hutchins, Pat. (1968). *Rosie's Walk* [illus]. New York: Simon & Schuster.

Jenkins, Steve. (1994). *Biggest, Strongest, Fastest* [illus by author]. Boston: Houghton.

Karas, G. Brian. (1993). *I Know an Old Lady* [illus]. New York: Scholastic.

Keats, Ezra Jack. (1983). *Peter's Chair* [illus]. New York: Harper Collins.

Kellogg, Steven. (1992). *The Christmas Witch* [illus by author]. New York: Dial.

Lester, Alison. (1993). *Isabella's Bed*. Boston: Houghton.

Lester, Helen. (1990). *Pookins Gets Her Way* [illus by Lynn Munsinger]. Boston: Houghton.

Lindbergh, Reeve. (1990). *Benjamin's Barn* [illus by Susan Jeffers]. New York: Dial.

Lobel, Arnold. (1973). *Frog and Toad are Friends* [illus]. New York: Harper Collins.

Lionni, Leo. (1994). *The Mixed-Up Chameleon* [illus by author]. New York: Greenwillow.

Lionni, Leo. (1974). *Alexander and the Wind Up Mouse* [illus by author]. New York: Random House.

McBratney, Sam. (1994). *Guess How Much I Love You* [illus by Anita Jeram]. Cambridge, MA: Candlewick.

Permission to reproduce

Mariotti, Mario. (1989). *Hanimations.* Brooklyn, NY: Kane-Miller.

Marshall, James. (1996). *Three Little Pigs* [illus]. New York: Penguin.

Martin, Jane Read & Patricia Marx. (1994). *Now Everybody Really Hates Me* [illus by Roz Chast]. New York: Harper Collins.

Martin Jr., Bill. (1993). *Chicka Chicka ABC.* Richmond Hill, ON: Distican.

Martin Jr., Bill. (1992). *Brown Bear, Brown Bear, What Do You See?* (25th Anniversary Edition) [illus by Eric Carle]. New York: Henry Holt.

Martin Jr., Bill and John Archambault. (1985). *The Ghost-Eye Tree* [illus by Ted Rand]. New York: Henry Holt.

Mayer, Mercer. (1975). *Just For You* [illus by author]. Racine, WI: Western.

Mayer, Mercer. (1977). *Just Me and My Dad* [illus]. Racine, WI: Western.

Mayer, Mercer. (1967). *A Boy, A Dog and a Frog* [illus by author]. New York: Dial.

Mollel, Tololwa M. (1992). *Promise to the Sun: A Story of Africa* [illus by Beatrice Vidal]. Boston: Little, Brown.

Mollel, Tololwa M. (1992). *Rhinos For Lunch and Elephants For Supper* [illus by Barbara Spurll]. Boston: Houghton Mifflin.

Munsch, Robert. (1993). *Wait and See* [illus by Michael Martchenko]. Toronto, ON: Annick.

Myller, Rolf. (1991). *How Big Is a Foot?* [illus by author]. New York: Dell.

Osofsky, Audrey. (1992). *Dreamcatcher* [illus by Ed Young]. New York: Orchard.

Palatini, Margie. (1994). *Piggie Pie!* [illus by Howard Fine]. New York: Clarion.

Pienkowski, Jan. (1982). *Robot* [illus by author]. New York: Delacorte. (Pop up book)

Potter, Beatrix. (1979). *The Tale of Peter Rabbit.* Mahwah, NJ: Troll Assoc.

Permission to reproduce

From Your Child's Teacher

Rathman, Peggy. (1995). *Officer Buckle and Gloria* [illus]. New York: Putnam.

Rathman, Peggy. (1992). *Ruby the Copycat* [illus by author]. New York: Scholastic.

Reid, Barbara. (1994). *Two By Two* [illus by author]. Richmond Hill, ON: Scholastic.

Rounds, Glen. (1994). *Sod Houses on the Great Plains* [illus]. New York: Holiday.

Rosen, Michael. (1994). *How Giraffe Got Such a Long Neck. And Why Rhino is So Grumpy* [illus by John Clementson]. New York: Dial.

Ryder, Joanne. (1991). *The Bear on the Moon* [illus by Carol Lacey]. New York: Morrow.

Rylant, Cynthia. (1991). *Henry and Mudge Take the Big Test* [illus by Sucie Stevenson]. New York: Bradbury.

Schertle, Alice. (1995). *Down the Road* [illus by E. B. Lewis]. San Diego: Harcourt/Browndeer.

Schoenherr, John. (1994). *Rebel* [illus by author]. New York: Putnam/Philomel.

Sendak, Maurice. (1963). *Where the Wild Things Are* [illus by author]. New York: Harper.

Serfozo, Mary. (1994). *Benjamin Bigfoot* [illus by Jos. A. Smith]. New York: Margaret K. McElderry Books.

Silsbe, Brenda. (1995). *The Watcher* [illus by Alice Priestly]. Toronto, ON: Annick.

Snyder, Dianne. (1991). *George and the Dragon Word* [illus by Brian Lies]. Boston: Houghton.

Stevenson, James. (1992). *Rolling Rose.* New York: Greenwillow.

Tafuri, Nancy. (1990). *Follow Me!* New York: Greenwillow.

Teague, Mark. (1992). *Frog Medicine* [illus by author]. New York: Scholastic.

Thayer, Jane. (1989). *The Popcorn Dragon* [illus by Lisa McCue]. New York: Morrow.

Tibo, Gilles. (1994). *Simon Finds a Feather* [illus by author]. Montreal, PQ: Tundra.

Permission to reproduce

Trivizas, Eugene. (1994). *The Three Little Wolves and the Big Bad Pig* [illus by Helen Oxenbury]. New York: Margaret K. McElderry Books.

Van Allsburg, Chris. (1990). *Polar Express* [illus by author]. Boston: Houghton

Ward, Heather P. (1994). *I Promise I'll Find You* [illus by Sheila McGraw]. Willowdale, ON: Firefly.

Wells, Rosemary. (1995). *Edward's Overwhelming Overnight* [illus by author]. New York: Dial.

Westcott, Nadine Bernard. (1980). *I Know an Old Lady Who Swallowed a Fly* [illus by author]. Boston: Little, Brown.

Willard, Nancy. (1991). *Pish, Posh, Said Hieronymus Bosch* [illus by Leo Dillon & Diane Dillon]. San Diego: Harcourt.

Williams, Vera B. (1984). *A Chair For My Mother* [illus]. New York: Greenwillow.

Wildsmith, Brian. (1981). *ABC*. Toronto, ON: Oxford University Press.

Wood, Audrey. (1988). *Elbert's Bad Word* [illus by author]. San Diego: Harcourt.

Young, Ed. (1995). *Donkey Trouble* [illus by author]. New York: Atheneum.

Permission to reproduce
From Your Child's Teacher

Ages Seven to Ten

Archer, Cheryl. (1994). *Snow Watch* [illus by Pat Cupples]. Toronto, ON: Kids Can Press. (Adventure)

Blume, Judy. (1970). *Are You There God? It's Me Margaret.* Scarsdale, NY: Bradbury. (Real-life issues)

Bogart, Jo Ellen. (1994). *Two Too Many* [illus by Yvonne Cathcart]. Richmond Hill, ON: North Winds Press.

Bradford, Karleen. (1994). *Thirteenth Child.* Toronto, ON: Harper Collins.

Brandenburg, Franz. (1984). *Leo and Emily and the Dragon.* [illus by Aliki]. New York: Greenwillow.

Brown, Marc. (1992). *Arthur Babysits* [illus by author]. Boston: Street, Brown.

Bruchac, Joseph. (1993). *Fox Song* [illus by Paul Morin]. Toronto, ON: Oxford University Press.

Bunting, Eve. (1989). *The Wednesday Surprise.* New York: Houghton.

Burnett, Frances Hodgson. (1987). *The Secret Garden* [illus by Graham Rust]. New York: Dilithium Press.

Byars, Betsy. (1985). *The Golly Sisters Go West* [illus by Sue Truesdell]. New York: Harper and Row.

Clearly, Beverly. (1983). *Dear Mr. Henshaw* [illus]. New York: Greenwillow.

Clearly, Beverly. (1975). *Ramona the Brave.* New York: Morrow.

Cooney, Barbara. (1982). *Miss Rumphius* [illus by author]. New York: Viking Press.

Counsel, June. (1984). *But Martin!* [illus by Carolyn Dinan]. London: Faber & Faber.

Dahl, Roald. (1982). *The BFG (Big Friendly Giant)* [illus by Quentin Blake]. New York: Penguin.

Dahl, Roald. (1961). *James and the Giant Peach* [illus by Nancy E. Burket]. New York: Knopf.

Dakos, Kali. (1994). *Don't Read This Book, Whatever You Do! More Poems About School* [illus by G. Brian Karas]. New York: Four Winds.

Permission to reproduce

Degen, Bruce. (1980). *The Little Witch and the Riddle* [illus by author]. New York: Harper & Row.

Delton, Judy. (1974). *Two Good Friends* [illus by Giulio Maestro]. New York: Crown.

Dorris, Michael. (1992). *Morning Girl.* New York: Hyperion.

Doyle, Brian. (1995). *Spud In Winter.* Toronto, ON: Groundwood Books.

Eyvindson, Peter. (1993). *The Missing Sun* [illus by Rhian Brynjolson]. Winnipeg, MB: Pemmican.

Fine, Jane. (1988). *Surprise!* [illus by Mary Morgan]. New York: Viking Kestrel.

Fitzhugh, Louise. (1965). *The Long Secret* [illus by author]. New York: Harper and Row.

Fitzhugh, Louise. (1964). *Harriet the Spy* [illus by author]. New York: Harper and Row.

Foreman, Michael. (1992). *One World* [illus by author]. New York: Arcade.

Fox, Paula. (1968). *The Stone-Faced Boy* [illus by Donald A. Mackay]. Englewood Cliffs, NJ: Bradbury.

Gifaldi, David. (1993). *The Boy Who Spoke Colors* [illus by C. Shana Greger]. Boston: Houghton.

Gilman, Phoebe. (1993). *Jillian Jiggs* [illus by author]. Toronto, ON: Scholastic.

Gilman, Phoebe. (1993). *Something From Nothing* [illus by author]. Toronto, ON: Scholastic.

Goble, Paul. (1994). *The Lost Children* [illus by author]. Englewood Cliffs, NJ: Bradbury.

Goennel, Heidi. (1988). *My Day* [illus by author]. Boston: Little.

Gordon, Jeffie Ross. (1992). *Two Badd Babies* [illus by Chris L. Demarest]. Honesdale, PA: Boyds Mills Press.

Greenwood, Barbara. (1994). *A Pioneer Story* [illus by Heather Collins]. Toronto, ON: Kids Can Press. (Award winner)

Heilbroner, Joan. (1962). *This is the House Where Jack Lives* [illus by Aliki]. New York: Harper.

Permission to reproduce

From Your Child's Teacher

Hoban, Lillian. (1985). *Arthur's Loose Tooth* [illus by author]. New York: Harper and Row.

Hutchins, Hazel. (1996). *Casey Webber the Great* [illus by John Richmond]. Toronto, ON: Annick.

Hutchins, Hazel. (1991). *Katie's Babbling Brother* [illus by Ruth Ohi]. Toronto, ON: Annick.

Iglotiorte, John. (1994). *An Inuk Boy Becomes A Hunter* [illus by author]. Halifax, NB: Nimbus.

James, Betsy. (1994). *The Mud Family* [illus by Paul Morin]. Don Mills, ON: Stoddart.

Kaner, Etta. (1995). *Towers and Tunnels* [illus by Pat Cupples]. Toronto, ON: Kids Can Press. (Activity)

Keens-Douglas, Ricardo. (1995). *Freedom Child of the Sea.* Toronto, ON: Annick.

Kellog, Steven. (1985). *Chicken Little* [illus by author]. New York: Greenwillow.

Kleitsch, Christel & Paul Stephens. (1985). *A Time to Be Brave.* Toronto, ON: Annick/Firefly.

Kushner, Donn. (1993). *A Thief Among Statues* [illus by Nancy Jackson]. Toronto, ON: Annick.

Lauber, Patricia. (1991). *Living with Dinosaurs* [illus by Douglas Henderson]. Englewood Cliffs, NJ: Bradbury.

Lawson, Julie. (1993). *Dragon's Pearl* [illus by Paul Morin]. New York: Clarion.

Lee, Dennis. (1974). *Alligator Pie* [illus by Frank Neufeld]. New York: Macmillan.

Levine, Ellen. (1994). *The Tree That Would Not Die.* [illus by Ted Rand]. New York: Scholastic.

Levine, Shar & Leslie Johnson. (1995). *Everyday Science: Fun And Easy Projects For Making Practical Things* [illus by Ed Shems]. New York: John Wiley & Sons. (Activity)

Lewis, C.S. (1961). *The Lion, the Witch and the Wardrobe* [illus by Pauline Baynes]. New York: Macmillan.

Lowry, Lois. (1989). *Number the Stars.* Boston: Houghton Mifflin.

Permission to reproduce

McDaniel, Becky B. (1987). *Katie Can* [illus by Lois Axeman]. Chicago: Children's Press.

McGugan, Jim. (1994). *A Prairie Boy's Story* [illus by Murray Kimber]. Red Deer, AB: Red Deer College Press. (Award winner)

MacLaughlin, Patricia. (1985). *Sarah Plain & Tall.* New York: Harper Collins.

Marshall, Edward. (1985). *Four on the Shore* [illus by James Marshall]. New York: Dial.

Marston, Sharyn. (1994). *Chinook.* Winnipeg, MB: Pemmican. (Folktale)

Michel, Francois. (1994). *Water Paper* [engineering by Francois Michel] [illus by Yves Larvor]. New York: Lothrop, Lee & Shepard.

Minarik, Else H. (1958). *No Fighting, No Biting!* [illus by Maurice Sendak]. New York: Harper & Row.

Mollel, Tololwa M. (1991). *Orphan Boy* [illus by Paul Morin]. Boston: Houghton Mifflin.

Morpurgo, Michael. (1991). *Waiting for Anya.* New York: Viking.

Myers, Laurie. (1994). *Earthquake in the Third Grade* [illus by Karen Ritz]. New York: Clarion.

Naylor, Phyllis Reynolds. (1992). *King of the Playground* [illus by Nola Langner Malone]. New York: Atheneum.

Numeroff, Laura. (1994). *Dogs Don't Wear Sneakers* [illus by Joe Mathieu]. New York: Simon and Schuster.

Parish, Peggy. (1966). *Amelia Bedelia and the Surprise Shower* [illus by Fritz Siebel]. New York: Harper and Row.

Park, Barbara. (1992). *Junie B. Jones and the Stupid Smelly School Bus* [illus by Denise Brunkus]. New York: Random House.

Park, Barbara. (1993). *Junie B. Jones and a Little Monkey Business* [illus by Denise Brunkus]. New York: Random House.

Perry, Sarah. (1995). *If ...* [illus]. Malibu, CA: J. Paul Getty Trust.

Ripley, Catherine. (1995). *Do Doors Open By Magic? And Other Supermarket Questions* [illus by Scot Ritchie]. Toronto, ON: Owl. (Non-fiction)

Permission to reproduce

Romain, Joseph. (1994). *Two Minutes for Roughing.* Toronto, ON: James Lorimer. (Sports)

Ross, Pat. (1983). *M and M and the Bad News Babies* [illus by Marylin Hafner]. New York: Pantheon.

Roy, Ron. (1979). *Awful Thursday* [illus by Lillian Hoban]. New York: Pantheon.

Saltzberg, Barney. (1984). *What To Say To Clara* [illus by author]. New York: Atheneum.

Schwartz, Alvin. (1985). *All of Our Noses are Here and Other Noodle Tales* [illus by Karen A. Winhaus]. New York: Harper and Row.

Scieszka, Jon. (1995). *Math Curse* [illus by Lane Smith]. New York: Viking. (Top of the List winner—Youth Picture Book)

Shannon, Margaret. (1994). *Elvira* [illus by author]. New York: Ticknor & Fields.

Silverstein, Shel. (1984). *Where the Sidewalk Ends.* New York: Random House.

Smucker, Barbara. (1995). *Selina and the Bear Paw Quilt* [illus by Janet Wilson]. Toronto, ON: Lester.

Spinelli, Jerry. (1992). *Fourth Grade Rats* [illus by Paul Casale]. New York: Scholastic.

Stanley, Fay. (1991). *The Last Princess: The Story of Princess Ka'iulani of Hawai'i* [illus by Diane Stanley]. New York: Four Winds.

Stevens, Carla. (1974). *Hooray for Pig!* [illus by Rainey Bennett]. New York: Seabury.

Steig, William. (1982). *Doctor De Soto.* New York: Harper Collins.

Tan, Amy. (1992). *The Moon Lady* [illus by Gretchen Schields]. New York: Macmillan.

Thomas, Colin. (1994). *Two Weeks, Twice A Year.* Victoria, BC: Scirocco. (Award winner)

Thomson, Pat. (1988). *Can You Hear Me, Grandad?* [illus by Jez Alborough]. New York: Delacorte.

Waddell, Martin. (1986). *The Tough Princess* [illus by Patrick Benson]. New York: Philomel.

Permission to reproduce

Wilder, Laura Ingalls. (1953). *Little House in the Big Woods* [illus by Garth Williams]. New York: Harper.

Williams, Margery. (1995). *The Velveteen Rabbit* [illus]. New York: Random House.

Wynne-Jones, Tim. (1992). *Zoom Away*. Toronto, ON: Groundwood.

Yee, Paul. (1996). *Ghost Train* [illus by Harvy Chan]. Toronto, ON: Groundwood.

Yolen, Jane. (1972). *The Girl Who Loved the Wind* [illus by Ed Young]. Toronto, ON: Harper Collins.

Zolotow, Charlotte. (1963). *The Quarreling Book* [illus by Arnold Lobel]. New York: Harper Collins.

Ages Eleven and up

Atkin, S. Beth. (1996). *Voices from the Streets: Young Former Gang Members Tell Their Stories* [photos by S. Beth Aitkin]. Boston: Little, Brown. (Real life issues, non-fiction)

Avi. (1996). *Beyond the Western Sea, Book One. The Escape from Home.* New York: Orchard. (Adventure)

Babbit, Natalie. (1975). *Tuck Everlasting.* New York: Farrar, Straus & Giroux. (Friendship)

Barron, T.A. (1996). *Lost Years of Merlin.* New York: Putnam.

Berry, Liz. (1996). *The China Garden.* New York: Farrar, Straus & Giroux.

Bode, Janet & Stan Mack. (1996). *Hard Time: A Real Life Look at Juvenile Crime* [illus by Stan Mack]. New York: Delacorte Press. (Non-fiction, real life issues)

Byars, Betsy. (1992). *Coast to Coast* [illus]. New York: Dell. (Travel/Adventure)

Cameron, Eleanor. (1990). *The Private World of Julia Redfern.* New York: New York: Penguin. (Real-life issues)

Carroll, Lewis. (1996). *Alice in Wonderland.* New York: Penguin.

Cart, Michael. (1996). *My Father's Scar.* New York: Simon & Schuster. (Real-life issues)

Chambers, Veronica. (1996). *Mama's Girl.* New York: Riverhead Books.

Chan, Gillian, (1994). *Golden Girl and Other Stories.* Toronto, ON: Kids Can Press.

Choi, Sook Nyul. (1991). *Year of Impossible Goodbyes.* Boston: Houghton Mifflin.

Choyce, Lesley. (1995) *Big Burn.* Saskatoon, SK: Thistledown. (Ecology)

Clark, Joan. (1995). *The Dream Carvers.* Toronto, ON: Viking.

Coles Jr., William. (1996). *Another Kind of Monday.* New York: Atheneum.

Conly, Jane Leslie. (1995). *Trout Summer.* New York: Henry Holt. (Family)

Permission to reproduce

Cooney, Caroline B. (1996). *The Voice on the Radio.* New York: Delacorte. (Family)

Cormier, Robert. (1994). *The Bumblebee Flies Anyway.* New York: Dell.

Creech, Sharon. (1994). *Walk Two Moons.* New York: Harper Collins.

Cushman, Karen. (1995). *The Midwife's Apprentice.* Boston: Houghton Mifflin.

Danakas, John. (1995). *Lizzie's Soccer Showdown.* Toronto, ON: James Lorimer. (Sports)

Dash, Joan. (1996). *We Shall Not Be Moved.* New York: Scholastic. (Non-fiction, historical)

Dessen, Sarah. (1996). *That Summer.* New York: Orchard. (Family)

Erbach, Janet. (1994). *Wanderer's First Summer.* Vancouver, BC: Polestar.

Farmer, Nancy (1996). *A Girl Named Disaster.* New York: Orchard.

Fleischman, Sid. (1996). *The Abracadabra Kid: A Writer's Life.* New York: Greenwillow. (Non-fiction, writing)

Fox, Paula. (1995). *The Eagle Kite.* New York: Orchard. (Real-life issues)

Fox, Paula. (1984). *The One-Eyed Cat* [illus by Irene Trivas]. New York: Simon & Schuster.

Freeman, Suzanne. (1996). *Cuckoo's Child.* New York: Greenwillow. (Family)

Gilstrap, John. (1996). *Nathan's Run.* New York: Harper Collins. (Mystery)

Glenn, Mel. (1996). *Who Killed Mr. Chippendale? A Mystery in Poems.* New York: Stewart. (Mystery)

Godfrey, Martyn. (1995). *It Seemed Like a Good Idea at the Time.* New York: Avon. (Friendship)

Godfrey, Martyn. (1992). *Great Science Fair Disaster.* New York: Scholastic.

Godfrey, Martyn. (1984). *Here She is Ms. Teeny Wonderful.* Richmond Hill, ON: Scholastic.

Permission to reproduce

Gould, Steven. (1996). *Wildside*. New York: Tom Doherty Assoc. (Fantasy)

Greene, Constance. (1991). *A Girl Called Al* [illus by Byron Barton]. New York: Penguin.

Greene, Constance. (1991). *I Know You Al*. New York: Penguin.

Haddix, Margaret Peterson. (1996). *Don't You Dare Read This, Mrs. Dunphrey*. New York: Simon & Schuster. (Real-life issues)

Haddix, Margaret Peterson. (1996). *Running Out of Time*. New York: Simon & Schuster. (Real-life issues)

Halvorson, Marilyn. (1986). *Cowboys Don't Cry*. New York: Dell.

Hanauer, Cathi. (1996). *My Sister's Bones*. New York: Delacorte.

Hautman, Pete. (1996). *Mr. Was*. New York: Simon & Schuster. (Family)

Hinton, S.E. (1971). *That Was Then, This is Now*. New York: Penguin. (Real-life issues)

Hinton, S.E. (1968). *The Outsiders*. New York: Dell. (Real-life issues)

Hobbs, Will. (1996). *Far North*. New York: Morrow.

Holeman, Linda. (1995). *Saying Goodbye*. Toronto, ON: Lester.

Hughes, Matt. (1994). *Fools Errant*. Don Mills, ON: Maxwell Macmillan.

Hughes, Monica. (1995). *My Name is Paula Popowich!* New York: James Lorimer.

Hughes, Monica. (1992). *Crystal Drop*. New York: Harper Collins.

Huth, Angela. (1996). *Land Girls*. New York: St. Martin's.

Ingold, Jeanette. (1996). *The Window*. San Diego: Harcourt.

Johnson, Julie. (1994). *Adam and Eve and Pinchme*. Toronto, ON: Lester.

Keillor, Garrison. (1996). *The Sandy Bottom Orchestra* [illus by Jenny Lind Nilson]. New York: Hyperion.

Kernaghan, Eileen. (1995). *Dance of the Snow Dragon*. Saskatoon, SK: Thistledown. (Fantasy)

Kipling, Rudyard. (1992). *The Jungle Book* [illus by Gregory Alexander]. New York: Arcade.

Permission to reproduce

Klass, David. (1996). *Danger Zone.* New York: Scholastic. (Sports)

Krakauer, Jon. (1996). *Into the Wild.* New York: Villard. (Non-fiction, adventure)

Lane, Dakota. (1996). *Johnny Voodoo.* New York: Delacorte.

Lawson, Julie. (1995). *Fires Burning.* Toronto, ON: Stoddart.

Levy, Marilyn. (1993). *Run for Your Life.* Boston: Houghton Mifflin.

Little, Jane. (1985). *Mama's Going to Buy You a Mockingbird.* New York: Penguin.

Lottridge, Celia Barker. (1995). *The Wind Wagon.* Toronto, ON: Groundwood.

Lowry, Lois. (1994). *The Giver.* Boston: Houghton Mifflin.

Lunn, Janet. (1983). *The Root Cellar.* New York: Simon & Schuster.

McNicoll, Sylvia. (1994). *Bringing Up Beauty.* Toronto, ON: Maxwell Macmillan. (Family)

Makris, Kathyrn. (1993). *Crosstown.* New York: Avon Flare.

Mead, Alice. (1996). *Adem's Cross.* New York: Farrar, Straus & Giroux. (Family)

Montgomery, Lucy Maud. (1942). *Anne of Green Gables.* Toronto, ON: Ryerson Press.

Myers, Walter Dean. (1996). *Slam!* New York: Scholastic. (Sports)

Naylor, Phyllis Reynolds. (1993). *Alice in April.* New York: Atheneum. (School)

Naylor, Phyllis Reynolds. (1991). *Shiloh.* New York: Simon & Schuster.

Nix, Garth. (1996). *Sabriel.* Toronto, ON: Harper Collins.

Nye, Naomi Shihab & Paul Janeczko. (1996). *I Feel a Little Jumpy Around You.* New York: Simon & Schuster. (Poetry)

Paterson, Katherine. (1996). *Jip, His Story.* New York: Stewart. (Historical)

Paterson, Katherine. (1991). *Lyddie Dutton.* New York: Dutton. (Historical)

Paterson, Katherine. (1977). *Bridge to Terabitha* [illus by Donna Diamond]. Toronto, ON: Harper Collins.

Permission to reproduce

Paulsen, Gary. (1989). *Hatchet*. New York: Penguin.

Pausewang, Gudrun. (1996). *The Final Journey*. Toronto, ON: Penguin.

Pearson, Kit. (1990). *The Sky is Falling*. Toronto, ON: Penguin.

Pearson, Kit. (1986). *The Daring Game*. Toronto, ON: Penguin.

Peck, Richard. (1992). *Don't Look & It Won't Hurt*. New York: Dell.

Peck, Richard. (1989). *Representing Super Doll*. New York: Dell.

Pennebaker, Ruth. (1996). *Don't Think Twice*. New York: Henry Holt. (Real- life issues)

Rising Voices: Writings of Young Native Americans. Selected by Arlene B. Hirshfelder and Beverly R. Singer. (1992). New York: Scribner's.

Salzman, Mark. (1995). *Lost in Place: Growing Up Absurd in Suburbia*. New York: Random House.

Savage, Candace. (1996). *Cowgirls*. Vancouver, BC: Ten Speed Press. (Non-fiction, Canadian west)

Schmidt, Gary D. (1996). *The Sin Eater*. New York: Stewart. (Adventure)

Southgate, Martha. (1996). *Another Way to Dance*. New York: Delacorte. (Real-life issues)

Spinelli, Jerry. (1996). *Maniac McGee* [illus]. New York: Harper Collins.

Staples, Suzanne Fisher. (1996). *Dangerous Skies*. New York: Farrar, Straus & Giroux. (Mystery)

Taylor, Cora. (1995). *Julie*. Vancouver, BC: Douglas & McIntyre.

Taylor, Cora. (1992). *Doll*. Vancouver, BC: Douglas & McIntyre.

Thesman, Jean. (1996). *The Ornament Tree*. Boston: Houghton, Mifflin.

Thomas, Rob. (1996). *Rats Saw God*. New York: Simon & Schuster.

Turner, Megan Whalen. (1996). *The Thief*. New York: Greenwillow. (Adventure)

Voight, Cynthia. (1981). *The Homecoming*. New York: Atheneum.

Permission to reproduce

Wallace, Rich. (1996). *Wrestling Sturbridge.* New York: Random House.

Welter, John. (1996). *I Want to Buy a Vowel.* Chapel Hill, NC: Algonquin.

Westall, Robert. (1996). *Gulf.* New York: Scholastic. (War)

White, Ruth. (1996). *Belle Prater's Boy.* New York: Farrar, Straus & Giroux. (Mystery)

Wieler, Diana. (1993). *Ran Van The Defender.* Toronto, ON: Groundwood.

Wilson, Budge. (1994). *Cordelia.* Clark Don Mills, ON: Stoddart.

The Authors

Robin Bright, BA, BEd, MEd, PhD

Robin is an Associate Professor in the Faculty of Education at the University of Lethbridge, where she instructs beginning teachers about the importance of literacy. She is the mother of two daughters whose own reading and writing development bring her joy and delight. Robin and her husband Glen also enjoy downhill skiing with their family.

Lisa McMullin, BEd, MEd

Lisa lives and works in Lethbridge. She has been an elementary teacher, a special education teacher, an assistant administrator, and an Elementary Liaison Counselor. Her personal and professional decision making is shaped by the commitment to live, to love, to learn, and to leave a legacy. Lisa's three children and husband Bruce keep her centered and grounded. She enjoys writing, yoga, walking, and planning adventures.

David Platt, BEd, DPE, MEd

David has taught full time since 1983. He earned his three Education degrees from the University of Lethbridge and is currently teaching Grade 6 at Mike Mountain Horse Elementary School in Lethbridge, Alberta. David, his wife Shari, and their two daughters Stacey and Ashley enjoy skiing and baseball.

Workshops! From Your Child's Teacher

Given by one or more of the authors, who are teachers as well as parents, this workshop can be targeted for teachers or parents.

Both workshops provide additional strategies and information that extend what is provided in this book.

For Teachers:

This workshop provides strategies for communicating what is happening in the classroom with regards to their children's development of literacy skills.

For Parents:

This workshop helps parents to understand the methodologies that teachers use in the classroom and gives them strategies for fostering literacy at home.

For more information or to book workshops, contact

4806–53 St.
Stettler, AB, Canada
T0C 2L2

Phone/Fax: 403-742-6483
Toll Free Phone/Fax: 1-888-374-8787
E-mail: hendriks@telusplanet.net
Website: www.telusplanet.net/public/hendriks

Distributed by:

Fitzhenry & Whiteside Publishers
195 Allstate Parkway
Markham, ON L3R 4T8
Phone: 905-477-9700, x.225
Fax: 905-477-9179

Toll Free Customer Service:
Phone: 800-387-9776, x.225
Fax: 800-260-9777
Email: godwit@fitzhenry.ca
Website: www.fitzhenry.ca

Liisa Moser

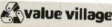

No need to buy expensive reading games. The best thing parents can do for their children at any age is to sit and read with them.

Discover

- strategies for making reading part of your child's life,
- helpful hints about reading with children,
- suggestions about what to read,
- strategies for helping your child develop as a writer,
- strategies for helping with homework, and
- answers to your reading development questions.

Packed with practical reading aids including reproducibles suitable for parent newsletters and book lists for children from birth to pre-teen.

"This book gives us a vision and a practical direction to break [the illiteracy] cycle so that all our children will have a fair chance to learn."

Senator Joyce Fairbairn, Special Advisor for Literacy

ISBN 0-96829-703-X

DYNAMIC YOU™

The Secret Code To Being Confident, Wealthy & Successful

Unleash your
Dynamic Woman™

DIANE ROLSTON